IMAGES
of Sport

THE AUSTRALIANS IN ENGLAND

Don Bradman takes the applause of the crowd as he leaves the ground at Headingley, Leeds in 1934.

IMAGES
of Sport

THE AUSTRALIANS
IN ENGLAND

Compiled by
William A. Powell

TEMPUS

Tempus Publishing Limited
The Mill, Brimscombe Port,
Stroud, Gloucestershire, GL5 2QG

ISBN 0 7524 1639 1

Typesetting and origination by
Tempus Publishing Limited
Printed in Great Britain by
Midway Colour Print, Wiltshire

This book is dedicated to my father-in-law John Stephen Curthoys (1940-2000), who was a fine sportsman both at Australian Rules football and cricket for his native Lalbert, Victoria.

The Australian cricket badge.

Contents

Acknowledgements

The author would like to thank the following, who have assisted in a variety of ways in the preparation of this book: Peter W.G. Powell, Mike Tarr, Stephen Waugh, John Ireland, John R. Lodge, the late Sir Donald Bradman AC, the late John Curthoys, Avis Curthoys, Carol Powell, Brian Curthoys, Michael Farrell, Sohail Malik, Dora Hall-Newman, John Eastwood, Martin Wood, Ian and Marie Huntington, Nicholas and Nicole Malik, Jamil and Elizabeth Malik, Ron Minto, Leonie McCrae, Sharon McCrae, Carl Rackemann, Lew and Peg Bond, the late Bill Martin and Loretta Martin, Geoffrey Lawson, Brian and Annabel Bassano, Don Wigan, Campbell Jamieson, Rick Smith, Ric Finlay, Gerry Wolstenholme, Mike Walsh, Mel Brown, Tony Sheldon, Bill Elliott, Murray Morrison, the late Ronald Harries and Dixie Harries, Doreen Moyes, Jamila and Michael Howarth, Keith Hayhurst, Ian Crawford, Mike Whitney, Ron and Merle Williams, Greg McKie, Irving Rosenwater, Bill Boiling, Vic and Jill Lewis, David Buxton, Kate Wiseman, Rosie Knowles, James Howarth and finally Justin Langer for his foreword to this book.

I acknowledge the sources of the illustrations, which are many and include in addition to those listed above the following: Stamp Publicity (Worthing) Limited, Patrick Eagar, Stuart Surridge, *The Cricketer*, National Sporting Club, Worcestershire CCC, Yorkshire CCC, Australian Cricket Board, Castlemaine XXXX, Neville Chadwick Photography, Middlesex CCC, Mark Sofilas, Kent CCC, Daily Express Newspapers, Surrey CCC, *Playfair Cricket Monthly*, Carreras, Caltex, JV Postcards, Bradman Museum, Victorian C.A., Deborah Wolstenholme, Lawsons, Essex CCC, Ken Kelly, George Bassett, Universal Pictorial Press, Derbyshire CCC, Scarborough C.C., Australian Broadcasting Corporation, T. Bolland, Walker Studios, Viyella Trousers, RA Postcards, Central News, Gripu Trousers, Jaeger Shirts, Marylebone C.C., S&G Press, Rotary Photography, Raphael Tuck, E. Hawkins & Co, Ivor Kerslake, F.C. Dick, Wrench Series and Playfair Books Ltd.

Other items are from my own collection of picture postcards, cigarette and trade cards and scorecards, magazines and newspapers. Apologies are offered to anyone whose photographs have inadvertently been used without acknowledgement.

Bibliography

Forty Seasons of First-Class Cricket by R.G. Barlow *His Career and Reminiscences* (John Heywood) 1900, *Australian Cricketers on Tour 1868-1974* by Les R. Hill (Lutheran Publishing, Adelaide) 1974, *The Complete History of Cricket Tours at Home and Abroad* by Peter Wynne-Thomas (Hamlyn) 1989, *Who's Who of Cricketers* by Philip J. Bailey, Philip Thorn and Peter Wynne-Thomas (Hamlyn) 1984, *The Oxford Companion to Australian Cricket* by Richie Benaud, Ian Chappell and Geoff Lawson (Oxford) 1996, *England v. Australia Test Match Records 1877-1985* by David Frith (Collins Willow) 1986, *The Encyclopaedia of Australian Cricket* by Malcolm Andrews (Golden Press) 1980, *A Complete Record of Australian Cricket Tours Home & Away* by Jack Pollard with statistics by Ross Dundas (ABC Books) 1995 and *The Top 100* and *The 1st XI* by Philip Derriman (The Fairfax Library) 1987.

Foreword

Sitting in the visitor's dressing room at Lord's in 1997, an interesting situation presented itself. Ever since I was a young boy, I have had a burning ambition to walk through the infamous Lord's Long Room wearing a baggy green cap. As I sat waiting for my turn to bat during the one day international, I looked down at my Australian helmet and batting gloves lying together at the foot of my chair. In an instant, it struck me that here was an opportunity to realise a childhood dream. Without thinking too much about the consequences of batting without my helmet, I walked over to my kitbag and replaced the modern protector with my cherished baggy green cap. At the time, it may have seemed a sign of arrogance to walk out and face the English fast bowlers without the more accepted means of batting headgear, but in reality my deed was more a matter of seizing the moment.

To most observers my actions may seem very insignificant, but in reality it goes deep to the core of why Australian cricket has such a rich history of achievement. Our cricket-loving nation undoubtedly has many assets which help to streamline our kids from backyard cricket to the Test team. A magnificent climate, incredible facilities, outstanding role models and a sport-mad culture encourage the masses to have a go at involving themselves in sport. This is all crucial to the past and continued development of Australian cricket; at a deeper level, the symbol of the baggy green cap has more significance than may be realised.

Within the current Australian cricket team there is a deep respect for the history of Australian cricket. As a symbolic gesture, initiated by our decorated captain Stephen Waugh, the team all wore replica 1900 baggy green caps during the First Test match of the new Millennium. As a respectful display to our predecessors of the last century, it was an honour to walk onto the Sydney Cricket Ground wearing the same cap that Victor Trumper and his team had worn one hundred years before.

From Sir Donald Bradman and Keith Miller to Dennis Lillee and Rodney Marsh, Australian cricket and the baggy green cap is steeped in fine tradition. This fantastic pictorial account of our history whilst touring in England, compiled by William Powell, depicts stories of courage, character and skill and shows off many of the heroes of our game.

Justin Langer
Western Australia Cricket Association, Middlesex County Cricket Club and Australia
May 2001

ESSEX v AUSTRALIANS

3 d. AT SOUTHCHURCH PARK, SOUTHEND-ON-SEA. **3 d.**

Sat, Mon, Tues, MAY 15, 17, 18, 1948.

* Captain † W-Kpr HOURS OF PLAY :- First 2 Days. 11.30-6.30. 3rd. 11-5.

INTERVALS   LUNCH :- 1.30-2.15   TEA 4.15-4.30 or according to state of game

UMPIRES Ashdown & Hendren   SCORERS Marshall & Ferguson   TOSS WON BY :- Australians

ESSEX.

		1st Innings		2nd Innings	
1	DODDS T C	c. Ring. b. Miller	0.	b. Toshack	16.
2	CRAY S J	b. Miller	5.	b. Johnson	15.
3	AVERY A V	b. Johnston	10.	c. Brown b. Johnson	3.
4	VIGAR F H	c. Saggers b. Miller	0.	c. Brown b. Toshack	0.
5	HORSFALL R	b. Toshack	11.	b. Johnson	8.
*6	T N PEARCE	c. Hamence b. Toshack	8.	c. b. Johnson	71.
7	T E BAILEY	ABSENT ILL	0.		0.
8	SMITH R	c. Barnes b. Toshack	25.	c. Ring. b. Johnson	0.
9	SMITH P	b. Toshack	3.	L.B.W. b. Barnes	54
†10	RIST F	c. Barnes b. Toshack	0.	b. Johnson	1.
11	PRICE E	NOT OUT	4.	NOT OUT	4.
	Extras	b-2 lb-6 nb-1 w-	9.	b-6 lb-3 nb-6 w-	15.
	TOTAL		**83**	**TOTAL**	**187**

FALL OF WICKETS

1st Innings	1	2	3	4	5	6	7	8	9	10	2nd Innings	1	2	3	4	5	6	7	8	9	10
	0	13	13	19	30	47	63	74	83	-		24	32	35	36	46	46	177	183	-	-

BOWLING ANALYSIS

	O	M	R	W	Wd	Nb	O	M	R	W	Wd	Nb
MILLER	8	3	14	3	0	0	2	1	4	0	0	
JOHNSTON	7	1	10	1	0	0	10	4	26	0	0	0
RING	11	4	19	0	0	0	7	3	16	0	0	0
TOSHACK	10.5	2	31	5	0	1	14	2	50	2	0	
JOHNSON							12.6	37	6	0		
LOXTON							12	3	29	0	0	
BARNES							9.4	5	11	1	0	

AUSTRALIANS

		1st Innings		2nd Innings
1	W A BROWN	c Horsfall b Bailey	153	
2	S G BARNES	hit wkt b Smith, R	79	
*3	D G BRADMAN	b Smith, P	187	
4	K R MILLER	b Bailey	0	
5	R HAMENCE	c Smith, P b Smith, R	46	
6	S LOXTON	c Rist b Vigar	120	
7	D RING	c Vigar b Smith, P	1	
8	I JOHNSON	st Rist b Smith, P	9	
†9	R SAGGERS	not out	104	
10	W A JOHNSTON	b Vigar	9	
11	E TOSHACK	c Vigar b Smith, P	4	
	Extras	b 7 lb- nb- 2 w-	9	b- lb- nb- w-
	TOTAL		721	TOTAL

FALL OF WICKETS

1st Innings	1	2	3	4	5	6	7	8	9	10
	145	364	364	452	499	664	686	692	716	721

BOWLING ANALYSIS

	O	M	R	W	Wd	Nb	O	M	R	W	Wd	Nb
Bailey	21	1	128	2								
Smith, R	37	2	169	2								
Smith, P	37	0	193	4								
Price	20	0	156	0								
Vigar	13	1	66	2								

AUSTRALIA WON BY AN INNINGS AND 451 RUNS

Completed scorecard of Essex versus Australians 1948 tour match at Southchurch Park, Southend-on-Sea when Australia scored 721 runs in one day.

The Australians of 1938 enjoy some free time in Europe.

Introduction

The 2001 season will see the 35th official Australian touring party of cricketers arrive and make a tour of our shores.

The first Australian tour was staged way back in 1878. Tours were made in 1880, 1882 and 1884, each one captained by Billy Murdoch. In 1886 the skipper of the touring party was H.J.H. Scott, while P.S. McDonnell was at the helm in 1888. In 1890 Billy Murdoch returned to captain the side and in 1893, 1896 and 1899 there were three different captains: J. McC. Blackham, G.H.S. Trott and Joe Darling.

After the turn of the century, Joe Darling was skipper for two further tours in 1902 and 1905. In 1909 Monte Noble led the touring side and in 1912 Syd Gregory led the Australians in the Triangular Test Series with England and South Africa. In 1921, after the intermission caused by the First World War, the Australians were led by Warwick Armstrong. In 1926 Herbie Collins was made captain, although Warren Bardsley did skipper the side in two Tests during the Series.

In 1930 and 1934 Bill Woodfull captained the side, while the legendary star batsman Don Bradman was at the helm on either side of the Second World War, in 1938 and 1948. During the 1950s and '60s, Australia were led by Lindsay Hassett in 1953, Ian Johnson in 1956, Richie Benaud and in one Test by Neil Harvey in 1961, Bobby Simpson in 1964 and by Bill Lawry and Barry Jarman in a single Test in 1968.

In 1972 and 1975 Ian Chappell led the baggy green caps before he handed over the captaincy to his younger brother, Greg, in 1977 and 1980. After Greg Chappell came Kim Hughes in 1981, who was followed by possibly the greatest Australian skipper since Don Bradman and Lindsay Hassett, 'A.B.' Allan Border captained the side in 1985, 1989 and 1993. Mark Taylor was captain in 1997 and his leadership saw the team win the 6 Test Series 3-2 with 1 draw, thus retaining the coveted Ashes Urn.

It is hoped that this book will evoke memories of previous Australian tours of this country by looking through this collection of historic pictures and viewing illustrations of some of the great teams, individual players, significant matches and performances which form part of the Australians' touring history in England.

William A. Powell
Hemel Hempstead, Hertfordshire
May 2001

A set of sixteen lapel badges issued by the Reno Theatre, South Kensington to celebrate the Australian cricket team as winners of The Ashes in 1934. Depicted in a clockwise direction from top left are: W.M. Woodfull, D.G. Bradman, W.H. Ponsford, S.J. McCabe, A.F. Kippax, W.A. Brown, W.A.S. Oldfield, C.V. Grimmett, T.W. Wall, L. O'B. Fleetwood-Smith, H.I. Ebeling, E.H. Bromley, L.S. Darling, B.A. Barnett, A.G. Chipperfield, W.J. O'Reilly.

The 1938 Australian touring party in Harrogate. After visiting a raincoat manufacturer in Yorkshire, each member was presented with a raincoat of their own. From left to right: C.W. Walker, W. Ferguson (scorer), J.H. Fingleton, W.A. Brown, A.G. Chipperfield, F.A. Ward, W.H. Jeanes (manager), E.L. McCormick, E.C.S. White, W.J. O'Reilly, L. O'B. Fleetwood-Smith, B.A. Barnett, M.G. Waite, S.J. McCabe, D.G. Bradman (captain), A.E. James (masseur), S.G. Barnes, C.L. Badcock, A.L. Hassett.

One

Early Tours 1878 to 1899

The team of 1878. From left to right, back row: J. McC. Blackham, T. Horan, G.H. Bailey, D.W. Gregory (captain), J. Conway (manager), A.C. Bannerman, C. Bannerman, W.L. Murdoch. Front row: F.R. Spofforth, F.E. Allen, W.E. Midwinter, T.W. Garrett, H.F. Boyle. The 1878 side played 17 first-class matches, winning 9, losing 4 and drawing 4. They also played 20 second-class matches, winning 9, losing 3 and drawing 8. No Test matches were staged during the first Australian tour of England. Charles Bannerman topped the tour batting averages with 566 runs (av. 20.96). With a top score of 61 he was, unsurprisingly, the leading run scorer. William Midwinter topped the bowling averages with 8 wickets (av. 7.25). Fred Spofforth was far the best bowler by far, taking 97 wickets (av. 11.00), with a best haul of 9 for 53.

John Blackham was born in North Fitzroy, Melbourne in 1854. An amateur, he was the brother-in-law of a fellow Victoria cricketer, G.E. Palmer, and played for the state 45 times between 1874/75 and 1894/95. A stubborn right-handed, lower-order batsman and brilliant wicketkeeper, he represented Australia in 35 Tests and captained his country in 8 Tests between 1876/77 and 1894/95. Blackham toured England in 1878, 1880, 1882, 1884, 1886, 1888, 1890 and 1893. In England he played 16 Tests, scoring 232 runs with a highest innings of 31 in the Third Test match at Kennington Oval in 1884. He held 13 catches and took 12 stumpings. In all Tests he scored 800 runs (av. 15.68), with a top score of 74, and he held 37 catches and took 24 stumpings. He was affectionately known as the 'Prince' of all Australia's early wicketkeepers as he was rather good at standing up to the wicket and striking the bails off with the ball to glove in one fell swoop. He died in Latrobe, Melbourne in 1932.

Alexander Bannerman was born in Paddington, Sydney in 1854. A right-handed opening batsman, right-arm medium pace round-arm bowler and fine fielder, he played 46 matches for his native New South Wales between 1876/77 and 1893/94. He later played 28 Tests for Australia between 1878/79 and 1893, during which time he toured England in 1878, 1880, 1882, 1884, 1888 and 1893. In England he played 11 Tests, scoring 291 runs, at an average of 15.32, with a highest score of 60 in the Third Test match at Old Trafford in 1893. He took 8 catches and 3 wickets at an average of 37.00, with a best performance of 3 for 111 at Kennington Oval in 1880. In his Test career he scored 1,108 Test runs (av. 23.08), with a highest innings of 94. He bagged 4 wickets (av. 40.75) and he held 21 catches. His brother was Charles who also represented Australia. He died in Paddington, Sydney in 1924.

Born in Balmain, Sydney in 1853, Fred Spofforth was one of the first right-arm fast-medium bowlers to appear in Australian cricket and was also a useful right-handed batsman. Known during his career as 'The Demon', he represented his native New South Wales from 1874/75 to 1897. A fine bowler when his team were in a crisis, he excelled on each of his tours to England in 1878, 1880, 1882, 1884 and 1886. He played 7 Tests in England and scored 65 runs (av. 7.22) with a top score of 20 not out in the First Test at Old Trafford in 1886. He also bagged 38 wickets (av. 17.13) with a best performance of 7 for 44 in the First Test at Kennington Oval in 1882. He played 18 Tests for Australia in all, taking 94 wickets (av. 18.41), with a best haul of 7 for 44 and he scored 217 runs (av. 9.43) with a top score of 50. He bagged 5 wickets in an innings 7 times and 10 wickets in a match 4 times. A follower of Anglo-Australian cricket, he represented Derbyshire in 9 county matches and also played club cricket for Hampstead CC in London in 1903. He was a successful businessman outside cricket, working as a tea merchant. The leading photographer of the time and pioneer of action photography, George Beldham, captured Spofforth's high leap as he delivered the ball – this picture is now firmly established in the history books. Spofforth died in Long Ditton, Surrey in 1926.

Born in Sydney in 1847, Henry Boyle was a lower order right-handed batsman and right-arm medium pace round-arm bowler. He represented Victoria in 28 matches between 1871/72 and 1887/88 and he played 5 of his 12 Tests in England, scoring 82 runs (av. 13.67) with a top score of 36 not out against England at Kennington Oval in 1880. He also bagged 16 wickets (av. 17.25) with a best haul of 6 for 42 at Old Trafford in 1884 and he held 3 catches. Boyle toured England in 1878, 1880, 1882, 1884, 1888 and 1890. His best tour was in 1882, when he bagged 125 wickets (av. 12.18). He died in East Bendigo, Victoria in 1907.

Born in St. Briavels, Gloucestershire in 1851, William Midwinter was a right-handed all-rounder and useful deep fielder. He toured England in 1878 and 1884, playing in 3 Tests. He scored 76 runs (av. 19.00) with a top score of 37 at Old Trafford in 1884, took a single wicket (av. 85.00) and he held 2 catches. He represented Victoria from 1874/75 to 1886/87 in 13 matches and played for Gloucestershire in 58 matches between 1877 and 1882. Midwinter is the only cricketer to have played for England in Australia and for Australia in England. In total he played 12 Tests, 8 for Australia between 1876/77 and 1886/87 and 4 for England in 1881/82. He died at Yarra Bend, Yew, Melbourne in 1890.

Born in Sandhurst in 1854, Bill Murdoch was a stylish middle order right-handed batsman and wicketkeeper who toured England in 1878, 1880, 1882, 1884 and 1890. Murdoch played 7 of his 18 Tests for Australia in England, scoring 497 runs (av. 45.18) with a top score of 211 at Kennington Oval in 1884 and also held 4 catches. He scored 153 not out at Kennington Oval in 1880 and exceeded 1,000 runs in a season on each of his tours of England, with a best performance of 1,582 runs (av. 31.64) in 1882. He also represented New South Wales from 1875/76 to 1893/94 in 19 matches, Sussex 1893 to 1899 in 137 matches, London County between 1901 and 1904 and England in a single Test in 1891/92. His highest score in England was 286 not out for the Australians versus Sussex at Hove in 1882. He captained Australia in 1880, 1882, 1884 and 1890, led Australia in 16 Tests and also captained Sussex between 1893 and 1899. He died in Melbourne in 1911.

Born in Kennington, London in 1858, Percy McDonnell was a fine right-handed attacking opening batsman and excellent slip fielder. He represented Victoria 14 times between 1877/78 and 1884/85, New South Wales 17 times between 1885/86 and 1891/92 and Queensland 3 times between 1894/95 and 1895/96. He toured England in 1880, 1882, 1884 and 1888. He played 7 of his 19 Tests in England, scoring 299 runs (av. 24.92) with a highest innings of 103 at Kennington Oval in 1884. His best bowling of 0 for 11 was achieved at Kennington Oval in 1880. His most successful tour of England was in 1888, when he accumulated 1,331 runs (av. 23.35). He died in South Brisbane, Queensland in 1896.

George 'The Colonial Hercules' Bonnor was born in 1855 in Bathurst, New South Wales. He was a right-handed all-rounder who was known for his extremely hard-hitting middle order batting performances and his medium pace bowling. He represented Victoria from 1881/82 to 1884/85 10 times and New South Wales between 1884/85 and 1890/91 in 5 matches. He toured England in 1880, 1882, 1884, 1886 and 1888. He played 10 of his 17 Tests in England, scoring 97 runs (av. 5.39) with a top score of 25 at Lord's, London in 1884. He also bagged 2 wickets (av. 30.50) with a best performance of 1 for 5 at Old Trafford in 1884. His best batting performance in England was for the touring Australians versus The Gentlemen at Lord's in 1888, when he hit a splendid 119. He died in East Orange, New South Wales in 1912.

George Giffen was born in Norwood, a suburb of Adelaide, in 1859. He was a right-handed all-rounder who played 13 of his 31 Tests in England, scoring 388 runs (av. 16.87) with a highest score of 80 at Old Trafford in 1896. He also took 33 wickets (av. 30.55) with a best haul of 7 for 128 at Kennington Oval in 1893 and held 7 catches. He toured England in 1882, 1884, 1886, 1893 and 1896. Giffen achieved the coveted double on the last of his three tours to England. His best tour was in 1886, when he amassed 1,424 runs (av. 26.86) and bagged 154 wickets (av. 17.36). Regarded by many as the W.G. Grace of Australian cricket, he achieved the unique record of 271 runs and 16 for 166 in the same match for South Australia versus Victoria at Adelaide in 1891/92. He died in Parkside, Adelaide in 1927.

The Australians in 1884. From left to right, back row: P.S. Mc.Donnell, G. Alexander (manager), G. Giffen, G.E. Palmer. Middle row: F.R. Spofforth, J. McC. Blackham, G.L. Murdoch, G.J. Bonnor, W. Midwinter, A. Bannerman, H.F. Boyle. Front row: W.H. Cooper, H.J.H. Scott. The 1884 Australian side played 31 first-class matches and won 17, lost 7 and drew 7. They also played and won 1 second-class match. The Test match series saw a 3-Test rubber with 0 wins, 1 loss and 2 drawn Tests.

The Australians in 1886. From left to right, back row: G. Giffen, F.R. Spofforth, Major Wardill (manager). Middle row: Farrands (umpire), Bates (scorer), W. Bruce, J. McIlwraith, T.W. Garrett, E. Evans, J.W. Trumble, Salter (scorer), Thoms (umpire). Front row: G.J. Bonnor, J. McC. Blackham, H.J.H. Scott, A.H. Jarvis, S.P. Jones, G.E. Palmer. The 1886 Australian side played 38 first-class matches, winning 9, losing 7 and drawing 21, with a single abandoned game. They also played and lost 1 second-class match. The Test Match Series saw a 3-Test rubber with 0 wins, 3 losses and 0 drawn Tests.

William Bruce was born in South Yarra, Melbourne in 1864. A left-handed all-rounder, he represented Victoria 61 times between 1882/83 and 1903/04. He toured England in 1886 and 1893, playing 5 of his 14 Tests in England. He scored 181 runs (av. 22.63) with a highest score of 68 at Old Trafford in 1893. He took 5 wickets (av. 34.80) with a best bowling performance of 2 for 26 at Old Trafford in 1893 and he held a total of 4 catches. His best tour of England was in 1893, when he amassed 1,227 runs (av. 25.01) with a highest innings of 191 for the Tourists versus Oxford and Cambridge Past and Present at the United Services Officers' Sports Ground, Portsmouth. He died in Elwood, St. Kilda, Melbourne in 1925.

The team of 1888. From left to right, back row: F.J. Ferris, S.P. Jones, A.H. Jarvis, J. Worrall, C.W. Beal (manager), J.J. Lyons, J. McC. Blackham, H.F. Boyle, J. Edwards. Front row: G.J. Bonnor, C.T.B. Turner, P.S. McDonnell (captain), H. Trott, A.C. Bannerman. The 1888 Australian side played 37 first-class matches, winning 17, losing 13 and drawing 7. They also played 3 second-class matches, winning 2 and losing 1. The Test match series saw a 3-Test rubber with 1 win, 2 losses and 0 drawn Tests.

The Australian team at Lord's in 1888. From left to right, back row: C.W. Beal (manager), A.H. Jarvis, J. Worrall, S.P. Jones, Farrands (umpire), J.J. Ferris, J. McC. Blackham, J. Edwards, C. Lord. Middle row: H.F. Boyle, C.T.B. Turner, P.S. Mc. Donnell (captain), A. Bannerman, S.J. Bonnor. Front row: J.J. Ferris, G.H.S. Trott.

Born in Collingwood, Melbourne in 1866, George Trott represented Australia in 11 of his 24 Tests in England and he toured in 1888, 1890, 1893 and 1896. He amassed 465 runs (av. 22.14) with a highest score of 143 at Lord's in 1896. He took 4 wickets (av. 49.25) with a best performance of 2 for 13 at Lord's in 1896 and he held 7 catches. A top order right-handed batsman, leg-break bowler and fine point fielder, he also represented his native Victoria in 59 matches between 1885/86 and 1907/08. His best tour of England was in 1896, when he accumulated 1,297 runs (av. 26.51). He died in Albert Park, Melbourne in 1917.

Born in Bathurst, New South Wales in 1862, Charles Turner played 8 of his 17 Tests in England, scoring 131 runs (av. 8.73) with a top score of 27 at Old Trafford in 1893. He took 38 wickets (av. 19.34) with a best performance of 6 for 67 at Lord's in 1893 and he held 3 catches. He toured England in 1888, 1890 and 1893. A forceful right-handed batsman and right-arm medium pace bowler, he bagged 283 wickets (av. 11.68) on tour in 1888, 179 wickets (av. 14.21) in 1890 and 148 wickets (av. 13.63) in 1893. His best bowling performance whilst on tour was 9 for 15 for the Australians versus An England XI at Stoke-on-Trent in 1888. He died in Manly, Sydney in 1944.

Born in Gawler, South Australia in 1863, John Lyons played 6 of his 14 Tests in England during his three tours in 1888, 1890 and 1893. He scored 293 runs (av. 26.64) with a highest innings of 55 at Lord's, London in 1890 and he took 5 wickets (av. 19.80) with a best haul of 5 for 30 at Lord's in 1890. He also took 2 catches. A right-handed all-rounder, he represented South Australia 47 times between 1894/95 and 1899/1900. His best tour of England was in 1893, when he amassed 1,377 runs (av. 28.10). He died in Magill, Adelaide in 1927.

Born in Sydney in 1867, John Ferris toured England in 1888 and 1890. A lower order left-handed batsman and medium left-arm bowler, he represented New South Wales in 19 matches between 1886/87 and 1897/98 and Gloucestershire in 63 matches between 1892 and 1895. Ferris played 5 of his 8 Tests for Australia whilst in England, scoring 89 runs (av. 12.71). He reached his top score of 20 not out at Lord's in 1888. He bagged 24 wickets (av. 14.08) with a best performance of 5 for 26 at Lord's in 1888 and held 3 catches. His best tour of England was in 1888, when he took 199 wickets (av. 14.74) and he made 1,056 runs (av. 22.46) in 1893. He played a single Test for England in 1891/92 and died in Durban, South Africa in 1900.

The team of 1890. From left to right, back row: H. Trumble, J. Mc.Blackham, K.E. Burn, Dr J.E. Barrett, H.F. Boyle. Middle row: F.H. Walters, G.H.S. Trott, W.L. Murdoch (captain), J.J. Lyons, C.T.B. Turner. Front row: S.E. Gregory, J.J. Ferris, P.C. Charlton, S.P. Jones. The 1890 Australian side played 35 first-class matches, winning 10, losing 16 and drawing 8. A single match was abandoned. They also played 4 second-class matches, winning 3 and losing 1. The Test match series saw a 3-Test rubber with 0 wins, 2 losses and 1 abandoned Test.

Hugh Trumble was born in Abbotsford, Melbourne in 1867. A right-handed middle order batsman, right-arm medium pace and off-break bowler and excellent slip fielder, he played 16 of his 32 Tests for Australia in England. Trumble scored 464 runs (av. 23.20) with a top score of 64 not out at Kennington Oval, London in 1902 and he took 67 wickets (av. 20.36) with a best haul of 8 for 65 at Kennington Oval also in 1902. He toured England in 1890, 1893, 1896, 1899 and 1902. Trumble was a prolific wicket-taker on tour in England and his tour records speak for themselves: he took 108 wickets (av. 16.61) in 1893, 148 wickets (av. 15.81) in 1896, 142 wickets (av. 18.43) in 1899 and 137 wickets (av. 14.02) in 1902. During the 1899 tour he also accumulated 1,183 runs (av. 27.51), thereby completing the coveted double. His best bowling return in England was 9 for 39 versus the South of England at Dean Park, Bournemouth in 1902. After retiring from the game he held the post of secretary of the Melbourne CC for 20 years until his death at Hawthorn, Melbourne in 1938.

Born in Randwick, Sydney in 1870, Syd Gregory was a right-handed middle order batsman, right-arm bowler and brilliant cover point fielder. He toured England in 1890, 1893, 1896, 1899, 1902, 1905, 1909 and 1912. He played 29 of his 58 Tests in England, scoring 888 runs (av. 19.73) with a highest innings of 117 at Kennington Oval in 1899 and he held 7 catches. Gregory represented his native New South Wales from 1889/90 to 1911/12 in 81 matches and accumulated 1,000 runs on 4 of his 8 tours of England, with a best performance of 1,464 runs (av. 31.95) in 1896. He died in the Moore Park district of Randwick, Sydney in 1929.

The team of 1893. From left to right, back row: Carpenter (umpire), Y. Cohen (manager), A.H. Jarvis, W.F. Giffen, W. Bruce, A.C. Bannerman, Thoms (umpire). Middle row: G.H.S. Trott, H. Trumble, G. Giffen, J. McC. Blackham (captain), J.J. Lyons, R.W. McLeod, C.T.B. Turner. Front row: H. Graham, A. Coningham, S.E. Gregory. The 1893 Australian side played 35 first-class matches, winning 17, losing 10 and drawing 8. They also played and won 1 second-class match. The Test match series saw a 3-Test rubber with 1 Test lost and 2 drawn.

Henry Graham was born in Carlton, Melbourne in 1870. A right-handed middle order batsman, leg-break bowler and good fielder, he played 4 of his 6 Tests in England during his tours in 1893 and 1896. Graham scored 180 runs (av. 25.71) with his highest score, 107, coming in his first Test at Lord's in 1893 and he also held 2 catches. He represented Victoria in 43 matches from 1892/93 until 1902/03 and Otago in New Zealand between 1903/04 and 1906/07. In 1893 he amassed 1,119 runs (av. 24.87) during the tour of England. He died in Dunedin, New Zealand in 1911.

The team of 1896. From left to right, back row: J. Darling, H. Trumble, A.E. Jones, H. Musgrove (manager), A.J. Eady, E. Jones, Thoms (umpire). Middle row: G. Giffen, R.R. McKibbin, G.H.S. Trott (captain), H. Donnan, F. Iredale. Front row: S.E. Gregory, J.J. Kelly, C. Hill. The 1896 Australian side played 34 first-class matches, winning 19, losing 6 and drawing 9. The Test match series saw a 3-Test rubber with 1 Test won and 2 lost.

Australian cricketers' autographs, dating from 1890 to 1910. This interesting collection includes Joe Darling, Monte Noble, Victor Trumper, Frank Iredale, Ernest Jones, Syd Gregory, Clem Hill, Hugh Trumble and Frank Laver.

24

Joe Darling played 18 of his 34 Tests for Australia in England during his tours in 1896, 1899, 1902 and 1905. He scored 683 runs (av. 22.77) with a highest innings of 73 at Old Trafford in 1905 and he held 9 catches. A left-handed top order batsman, slow bowler and good fielder, he was born in the Glen Osmond suburb of Adelaide in 1870 and he represented South Australia in 42 matches from 1893/94 to 1907/08. Darling captained Australia in England in 1899, 1902 and 1905 and he achieved 1,000 runs in all of his tours to England, with a best summer of 1,941 runs (av. 41.29) in 1899. He was later a Tasmanian parliament minister from 1921 until his death in Hobart, Tasmania in 1946.

Clement 'Clem' Hill was born in Hindmarsh, Adelaide in 1877. A left-handed top order batsman and leg-break bowler, he represented his native South Australia 87 times between 1892/93 and 1922/23. Hill toured England in 1896, 1899, 1902 and 1905 and played 16 of his 49 Tests in England, scoring 777 runs (av. 28.78) and holding 9 catches, with a highest score of 135 at Lord's in 1899. He achieved 1,000 runs on 3 of his tours of England, with a best of 1,722 runs (av. 38.26) in 1905. He died from injuries received when he was thrown from a moving tram after it had been involved in an accident in Parkville, Melbourne in 1945.

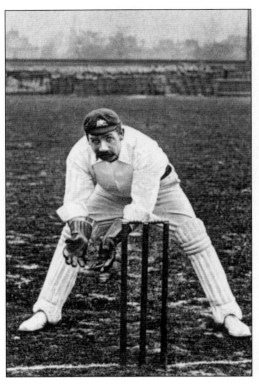

James Kelly, a lower right-handed batsman and wicketkeeper, was born in Port Melbourne, Victoria in 1867. He represented Australia in 18 of his 36 Tests during tours of England in 1896, 1899, 1902 and 1905. He amassed 309 runs (av. 18.18) with a top score of 42 at Kennington Oval in 1905 and he also attained 25 dismissals (16 catches and 9 stumpings). Despite being born in Victoria, Kelly represented New South Wales 53 times from 1894/95 to 1904/05. He died in Bellevue Hill, New South Wales in 1938.

Montague 'Monty' Noble was born in Chinatown, Sydney in 1873. He represented New South Wales between 1893/94 and 1919/20 77 times as a right-handed middle order batsman, right-arm medium pace off-break bowler and brilliant fielder. He toured England with Australia in 1899, 1902, 1905 and 1909. He played 20 of his 42 Tests in England scoring 848 runs (av. 26.50) with a highest innings of 89 at Old Trafford in 1899, bagged 37 wickets (av. 33.51) with a best haul of 6 for 52 at Bramall Lane, Sheffield in 1902 and he held 9 catches. He reached 1,000 runs on each of his tours of England with a best of 2,053 runs (av. 46.65) in 1905. His highest individual innings was 284 for the touring Australians versus Sussex at Hove in 1896. He became a respected cricket writer and was the brother-in-law of William Ferguson, the tourists' scorer and baggage master. He died in Randwick, Sydney in 1940.

Born in Darlinghurst, Sydney in 1877, Victor Trumper was a brilliant right-handed top order batsman and right-arm medium pace bowler. He represented New South Wales 73 times between 1894/95 and 1913/14 and he toured England 4 times in 1899, 1902, 1905 and 1909. He scored 863 runs (av. 27.84) with a highest score of 135 not out at Lord's in 1899 and he also took 2 wickets (av. 50.00) with a best performance of 2 for 35 at Edgbaston, Birmingham in 1902 and he held 7 catches. He achieved 1,000 runs on each of his tours to England, with a best season of 2,570 runs (av. 48.49) in 1902. His highest individual innings in England was 300 not out versus Sussex at Hove in 1899. He died in Darlinghurst, Sydney in 1915.

Frank Laver was born in Castlemaine, Victoria in 1869. A right-handed middle order batsman with a most unusual style, right-arm medium pace bowler and splendid point fielder he represented Victoria 78 times between 1891/92 and 1911/12. Laver toured England 3 times in 1899, 1905 and 1909. He played 13 of his 15 Tests in England, scoring 180 runs (av. 13.85) with a highest score of 45 at Headingley in 1899. He also took 34 wickets (av. 22.62) with a best performance of 8 for 31 at Old Trafford in 1909 and held 6 catches. His most successful tour of England was in 1905, when he took 115 wickets (av. 18.19). He also acted as player-manager of the tour and his subsequent tour of England in 1909. A well respected cricket writer, his book *An Australian Cricketer on Tour* was published in 1905. He died in East Melbourne, Victoria in 1919.

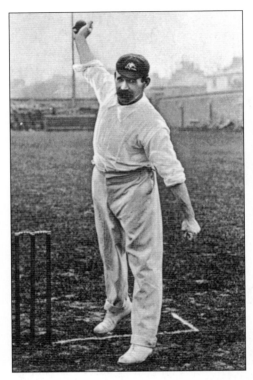

Born in Penrith, New South Wales in 1869, William Howell toured England in 1899, 1902 and 1905. He played 6 of his 18 Tests whilst in England, scoring 17 runs (av. 2.83) with a top score of 7 at Headingley in 1899. He took 9 wickets (av. 44.89) with a best performance of 2 for 43 at Trent Bridge in 1899 and he held a single catch. In 1899 he bagged 10 for 28 against Surrey at Kennington Oval, London and finished the tour that year with 117 wickets (av. 20.35). He died in Castlereagh, Sydney in 1940.

Charles McLeod toured England in 1899 and 1905 and he played 6 of his 17 Tests for Australia in England. He scored 155 runs (av. 19.38) with a top score of 77 at Kennington Oval in 1899 and he bagged 11 wickets (av. 59.64) with a best haul of 5 for 125 at Old Trafford in 1905 and he held a single catch. Born in Port Melbourne in 1869, he represented Victoria 41 times between 1893/94 and 1903/04 as a right-handed opening batsman and right-arm medium pace bowler. He died in the Toorak district of Melbourne in 1918.

Two

The Golden Age of the Baggy Green Caps 1902 to 1912

The Australians of 1902. From left to right, back row: W.P. Howell, C. Hill, H. Trumble, Major Wardill (manager), W.W. Armstrong, E. Jones, A.J.Y. Hopkins, R.A. Duff. Middle row: V.T. Trumper, M.A. Noble, J. Darling (captain), J.V. Saunders, J.J. Kelly. Front row: H. Carter, S.E. Gregory. The 1902 Australian side played 38 first-class matches, winning 22, losing 2 and drawing 14. They also played and won 1 second-class match. The Test match series saw a 5-Test rubber for the first time during a tour of England. The series ended with 1 Test won and 4 lost.

Born in 1878 in Sydney, Reginald Duff was a right-handed opening batsman and right-arm medium pace bowler. He represented New South Wales from 1898/99 to 1907/08 in 38 matches and toured England in 1902 and 1905. He played 10 of his 22 Tests in England, scoring 464 runs (av. 29.00) with a highest innings of 146 at Kennington Oval in 1905. He took 4 wickets (av. 21.25) with a best performance of 2 for 43 at Trent Bridge in 1905 and he also held 7 catches. Duff reached 1,000 runs on each of his England tours, with a best of 1,403 runs (av. 22.50) in 1902. He achieved the feat of scoring a century on both his Test debut and in his final Test appearance. He died of alcoholism in North Sydney in 1911.

Warwick Armstrong toured England in 1902, 1905, 1909 and 1921. He played 20 of his 50 Tests whilst in England, scoring 690 runs (av. 24.64). His highest score of 77 was achieved at Headingley in 1921. He took 40 wickets (av. 29.15), with a best performance of 6 for 35 at Lord's in 1909 and he also held 22 catches. Born in Kyneton, Victoria in 1879, he was a right-handed middle-order batsman and originally a right-arm fast-medium bowler but later turned to leg-breaks. He represented Victoria 83 times between 1898/99 and 1921/22, but he performed of his best in England. On three of his four tours to England he achieved the coveted double of 1,000 runs and 100 wickets. His best tour was in 1905, when he achieved 1,902 runs (av. 50.05) and bagged 122 wickets (av. 18.20). His physique was massive he was over 6 foot tall and weighed in at 20 stone and he was known to all those in the game as 'The Big Ship'. The Somerset side who represented the county at Bath in 1905 can vouch for that, as Armstrong amassed a mammoth ground record individual innings of 303 not out against the home side for the touring Australians. The Australians' total of 609 for 4 declared is still the highest innings total against Somerset on the ground in a first-class match. Armstrong died in Sydney in 1947.

Born in Young, New South Wales in 1874, Albert Hopkins toured England in 1902, 1905 and 1909. A sound right-handed top order batsman and right-arm fast-medium bowler, he represented New South Wales 52 times between 1896/97 and 1914/15. He played 10 of his 20 Tests in England, scoring 230 runs (av. 16.43) with a top score of 40 not out at Bramall Lane, Sheffield. He took 10 wickets (av. 28.60) with a best performance of 3 for 40 at Lord's in 1905 and he also held 4 catches. His best tour of England was without doubt in 1902, when he scored 1,100 runs and took 34 wickets. He died in North Sydney in 1931.

Born in Halifax, Yorkshire in 1878, Hanson Carter toured England in 1902, 1909 and 1921. A lower order right-handed batsman and wicketkeeper, he represented New South Wales from 1897/98 to 1924/25 44 times. He played 9 of his 28 Tests against England in England, scoring 228 runs (av. 17.54). His highest score was 47, made at Headingley in 1921 and he achieved 21 dismissals (14 catches and 7 stumpings). Regarded by the Australian public as the best wicketkeeper to have represented the baggy green caps since Jack Blackham, he died in the Bellevue district of Sydney in 1948.

The Australian tourists take to the field at Lord's during the Second Test match with England in 1905.

Born in Sydney in 1884, Albert 'Dibby' Cotter was a lower order right-handed batsman and right-arm fast bowler. He played 38 matches for his native New South Wales from 1901/02 to 1913/14 and also toured England in 1905 and 1909. Cotter played 8 of his 21 Tests for Australia in England, scoring 146 runs (av. 11.23). His highest innings, 45, was reached at Trent Bridge in 1905. He took 30 wickets (av. 26.40) with a best performance of 7 for 148 at Kennington Oval in 1905 and he held 3 catches. His best tour of England was his first, in 1905, when he bagged 119 wickets (av. 20.41). He died from injuries sustained while acting as a stretcher-bearer during the First World War and was buried approximately 2 miles south of Beersheba in Palestine in 1917.

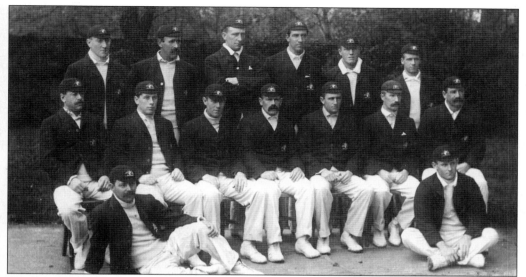

The Australian team of 1905. From left to right, back row: D.R.A. Gehrs, W.P. Howell, W.W. Armstrong, F. Laver (manager), A.J.Y. Hopkins, P.M. Newland. Middle row: R.A. Duff, C.Hill, V.T. Trumper, J. Darling (captain), M.A. Noble (vice-captain), C.E. McLeod, J.J. Kelly. Front row: S.E. Gregory, A. Cotter. The 1905 Australian side played 37 first-class matches, winning 16, losing 3 and drawing 18. They also played and drew 1 second-class match. The Test match series saw a 5-Test rubber with 0 wins, 2 losses and 3 drawn Tests.

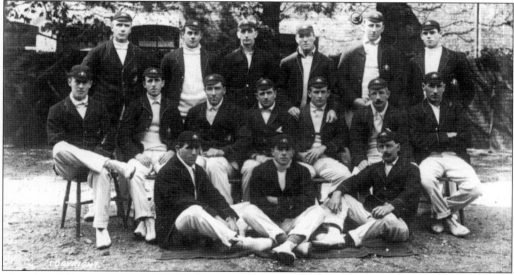

The Australian team in 1909. From left to right, back row: P.A. McAlister, W. Bardsley, R.J. Hartigan, A.J.Y. Hopkins, W.W. Armstrong, W.J. Whitty. Middle row: V.T. Trumper, VS. Ransford, F. Laver, M.A. Noble (captain), A. Cotter, H. Carter, J.D.A. O'Connor. Front row: W. Carkeek, C.G. Macartney, S.E. Gregory. The 1909 Australian side played 37 first-class matches, winning 11, losing 4 and drawing 22. They also played 2 second-class matches, winning both. The Test match series saw a 5-Test rubber, with 2 Tests won, 1 lost and 3 drawn. This was only the second touring Australian side to achieve an Ashes series victory in England, the first having taken place in 1882.

The Australians take to the field at Uttoxeter, Staffordshire on 6 September 1909, where a match was staged with Mr J. Bamford's XI. The match was drawn, Mr J. Bamford's XI making 140 and the Australians 110 for 7. J.D.A. O'Connor took match figures of 6 for 42 for the Australians. Mr John Bamford was a leading industrialist whose family later developed the JCB (J.C. Bamford) back-acter piece of machinery, which is commonly used on building and civil engineering construction sites around the world.

Warren Bardsley was born in Warren, New South Wales in 1882. A stylish, left-handed top order batsman, he represented New South Wales 83 times between 1903/04 and 1925/26 and he toured England with Australia in 1909, 1912, 1921 and 1926. Bardsley played 18 of his 41 Tests in England for Australia, during which time he accumulated 959 runs (av. 41.70), with a highest score of 193 not out at Lord's in 1926 and he held 3 catches. Bardsley also scored 2 hundreds in the same Test at Kennington Oval in 1909, when he hit 136 and 130. In 1926 Bardsley scored 193 in the Lord's Test of that summer, which was the highest individual innings recorded in a Test at cricket headquarters until it was beaten by Don Bradman. Bardsley died in the Bondi district of Sydney in 1954.

Born in West Maitland, New South Wales in 1886, Charlie Macartney was a right-handed attacking middle-order batsman, slow-left arm bowler and fine fielder. He represented New South Wales 81 times between 1905/06 and 1926/27 and he toured England in 1909, 1912, 1921 and 1926. He played 18 of his 35 Tests in England, scoring 1,054 runs (av. 45.83) with a highest innings of 151 at Headingley in 1926. He also bagged 22 wickets (av. 26.41) with a best bowling performance of 7 for 58 at Headingley in 1909 and he also held 8 catches. His best tour of England came in 1921, when he amassed 2,317 runs (av. 59.42) including a ground record breaking 345 against Nottinghamshire at Trent Bridge. He also recorded 2,000 runs in 1912 and topped 1,000 runs in 1926. Whilst in England he amassed three other scores of over 200, including one against Essex in 1912. He died in Little Bay, Sydney in 1958.

The Australian cricketers in England for the Triangular Test Series with England and South Africa in 1912. From left to right, back row: C.J. Crouch (manager), R.B. Minnett, E. Hume (visitor), C. Kelleway, E.R. Mayne, S.H. Emery, D.B.M. Smith, W.J. Whitty, H.W. Webster, G.R. Hazlitt. Front row: W. Bardsley, J.W. McLaren, T.J. Matthews, S.E. Gregory (captain), C.B. Jennings (vice-captain), C.G. Macartney, W. Carkeek. The 1912 Australian side played 36 first-class matches, winning 9, losing 8 and drawing 19. They also played 2 second-class matches with 1 drawn and 1 abandoned. The Test match series saw a 5-Test rubber with 2 wins, 1 loss and 3 drawn Tests.

Three

Armstrong's Australians 1921 to 1930

The 1921 Australians. From left to right, back row: W. Bardsley, J.S. Ryder, H.S.T.L. Hendry, J.M. Gregory, E.R. Mayne, T.J.E. Andrews, S. Smith (manager). Middle row: A.A. Mailey, E.A. McDonald, H.L. Collins, W.W. Armstrong (captain), C.G. Macartney, H. Carter, J.M. Taylor. Front row: C.E. Pellew, W.A.S. Oldfield. The 1921 Australian side played 34 first-class matches, winning 21, losing 2 and drawing 11. They also played 4 second-class matches, winning 1 and drawing 4. The Test match series saw a 5-Test rubber with 3 wins, 0 losses and 2 draws.

Gregory practising slows

The Australians at Leicester!

Macartney as kerky as ever

Hendry is the Adonis of the Team

Ryder

McDonald

Mailey

18 stones of cricket & geniality

Bardsley looks more than ever like Geo: Robey

Rip!

A cartoon of the Australians at Aylestone Road, Leicester by a contemporary artist of the time, Rip. It depicts the 20 stone Australian skipper Warwick Armstrong from Kyneton plus some of his team-mates on the 1921 tour of England.

The victorious 1921 Australians, pictured at the Hotel Cecil, London on 30 September 1921 prior to the team's departure for Australia by boat. The proceeds of the sale of this postcard were given to the Funds of the Royal Free Hospital, situated in Gray's Inn Road, London, which was established in 1828 to help the poor and the sick. The Australians, led by Warwick Armstrong, played a total of 38 matches during the tour, winning 22, drawing 14 and losing just 2.

Touring England in 1921 and 1926, Jack Gregory played 10 of his 24 Tests in England. He scored 275 runs (av. 22.92) with a top score of 73 at Kennington Oval in 1926. He bagged 22 wickets (av. 38.64) with a best performance of 6 for 58 at Trent Bridge in 1921 and he held 9 catches. Gregory was born in North Sydney in 1895 and he represented New South Wales as a left-handed top order batsman and right-arm fast-medium bowler in 17 matches between 1920/21 and 1928/29. His best tour of England came when he bagged 116 wickets (av. 16.58) in 1921. His opening bowling partnership with Ted McDonald on the 1921 tour was the equal of any pair of opening bowlers at the time. In 1927 he married the then Miss Australia. He died in Bega, New South Wales in 1973.

Born in Newtown, New South Wales in 1890, Thomas Andrews toured England in 1921 and 1926. He represented Australia in 10 of his 16 Tests in England, scoring 324 runs (av. 24.92), with a top score of 94 at Kennington Oval in 1921. His bowling performance was less striking – he took a single wicket (av. 116.00) with a best performance of 1 for 23 at Old Trafford in 1921 and he held 6 catches. An attractive, right-handed middle order batsman, leg-break and googly bowler, he played 74 matches for New South Wales between 1912/13 and 1928/29. His highest score was 247 not out for New South Wales versus Victoria at the Sydney Cricket Ground in 1919/20. He died in Croydon, Sydney in 1970.

Born in Darlinghurst, Sydney in 1889, Herbert 'Herbie' Collins was a sound right-handed top order batsman and slow left-arm bowler. He played 52 games for New South Wales between 1909/10 and 1925/26 and went on tour with Australia to England in 1921 and 1926. He played 6 of his 19 Tests in England, scoring 161 runs (av. 23.00) with a highest innings of 61 at Kennington Oval in 1926 and he held 2 catches. His best bowling performance was 0 for 11 at Lord's in 1926. He skippered the tourists in 1926 and in total he captained his country in 11 of his 19 Tests. His highest innings in domestic cricket was 282 for New South Wales versus Tasmania at Hobart in 1912/13,and his best score in Test cricket was 203 against South Africa at Johannesburg in 1921/22. He died in Little Bay, Sydney in 1959.

Born in Alexandria, Sydney in 1894, William 'Bertie' Oldfield, Australia's wicketkeeper for the tours of England in 1921, 1926, 1930 and 1934, was a commanding figure behind the stumps. He played 82 matches between 1919/20 and 1937/38 for New South Wales in domestic Australian cricket. He also played 16 of his 54 Tests in England, during which time he amassed 344 runs (av. 22.93) with a highest score of 43 not out at Lord's in 1930 and he achieved 37 dismissals (26 catches and 11 stumpings). Regarded as the best wicketkeeper since Blackham and Carter to wear the gloves for the Australians, he was without doubt the best of his generation behind the timbers. He was awarded the MBE for services to Australian cricket and he died in the Killara district of Sydney in 1976.

Touring England just once, in 1921, Ted McDonald was born in Launceston, Tasmania in 1891. He played 5 of his 11 Tests in England, scoring 92 runs (av. 46.00) with a highest innings of 36 at Kennington Oval in 1921. He also bagged 27 wickets (av. 24.74) with a best haul of 5 for 32 at Trent Bridge in 1921 and he held a single catch. McDonald represented Tasmania between 1909/10 and 1910/11 in 2 games and Victoria between 1911/12 and 1921/22 in 22 matches. However, the majority of his games were played for Lancashire, whom he represented 217 times between 1924 and 1931. In 1921 he bagged 138 wickets (av. 16.55), but he topped that in 1925 when he took a mammoth 205 wickets (av. 18.66), when he returned to England to represent Lancashire. A noted Australian rugby and soccer footballer, he died in Blackrod a district of Bolton in Lancashire in 1937 when he was tragically killed in a road accident.

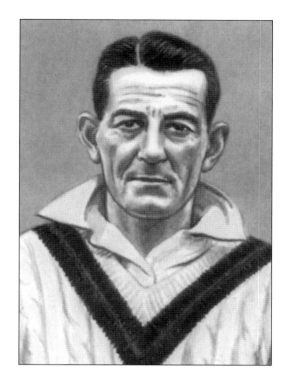

Known for his excellent cartoon drawings, his splendid writing on the game of cricket and his fine bowling performances, Arthur Mailey was born in Sydney in 1886 and toured England in 1921 and 1926. Mailey represented New South Wales 67 times as a lower order right-handed batsman and leg-break and googly bowler between 1912/13 and 1929/30. He played 8 of his 21 Tests in England for Australia, scoring 20 runs (av. 2.86) with a highest score of 6 at Headingley in 1921 and again at Kennington Oval in 1926, and he held 2 catches. On his first tour of England in 1921 he bagged 134 wickets (av. 19.36) and on his second, in 1926, he bagged 126 wickets (av. 19.34). His best bowling performance came at Cheltenham College for the touring Australians against Gloucestershire, when he took all 10 county wickets for the princely sum of 66 runs. He died in the Kirrawee district of Sydney in 1967.

Representing Australia in England twice in 1921 and 1926, Johnny Taylor was born in Stanmore, Sydney in 1895. He was a right-handed middle order batsman and brilliant cover point fielder who represented New South Wales from 1913/14 to 1926/27 in 27 matches. He played 8 of his 20 Tests on English soil scoring 186 runs (av. 23.25) with a highest innings of 75 at Kennington Oval in 1921 and he held 2 catches. His bowling saw a single wicket attained (av. 26.00), with a best performance of 1 for 25 at Kennington Oval in 1921. His best tour of England was in 1921, when he just managed to reach 1,000 runs in first-class games on the tour. He died in Turramurra, Sydney in 1971.

The Australians and Sussex players pictured together at the County Cricket Ground, Hove on 30 August 1926. Australians 367 (A.F. Kippax 158, A. Hurwood 61, P.M. Hornibrook 59 not out, M.W. Tate 6 for 82) and 233 for 9 declared (A.F. Kippax 102 not out) drew with Sussex 269 (J.H. Parks 84, T. Cook 67 not out, P.M. Hornibrook 5 for 51) and 93 for 1.

The team of 1926. From left to right, back row: J.L. Ellis, A.L. Hendry, J.M. Gregory, J.S. Ryder, A.J. Richardson, S.G. Everitt, S. Smith (manager). Middle row: A.A. Mailey, C.V. Grimmett, W. Bardsley (vice-captain), H.L. Collins (captain), C.G. Macartney, T.J.E. Andrews, J.M. Taylor. Front row: W.M. Woodfull, W.H. Ponsford, W.A.S. Oldfield. The 1926 Australian side played 33 first-class matches, winning 9, losing 1 and drawing 23. They also played 7 second-class matches with 3 wins and 4 draws. The Test match series saw a 5-Test rubber with 0 wins, 1 loss and 4 drawn Tests.

Born in Maldon, Victoria in 1897, Bill Woodfull was a right-handed opening batsman who tended to play in a defensive manner. He represented Victoria 59 times between 1921/22 and 1933/34 and captained Australia on the latter two of his three tours of England in 1926, 1930 and 1934. He played 15 of his 35 Tests in England, scoring 879 runs (av. 43.95) with a highest score of 155 at Lord's in 1930. During the 1926 tour he made 2 Test centuries, 141 at Headingley and 117 at Old Trafford. He amassed 1,000 runs on each of his visits to England, with a best tour performance of 1,672 runs (av. 57.65) in 1926. His highest individual innings on tour in England was his 228 not out, which was recorded against Glamorgan at St. Helen's Ground, Swansea in 1934. He collapsed and died whilst playing golf at Teed Heads South, New South Wales in 1965.

Bill Ponsford was born in North Fitzroy, Melbourne in 1900 and he represented Victoria 55 times as a right-handed opening batsman and right-arm medium pace bowler between 1920/21 and 1933/34. He toured England three times with Australia in 1926, 1930 and 1934 and represented the baggy green caps in 10 of his 29 Tests in England, scoring 936 runs (av. 62.40) with a highest innings of 266 at Kennington Oval in 1934 and he held 8 catches. In 1930 he amassed 110 at Kennington Oval and in 1934 he went 71 runs better when he scored 181 at Headingley. Ponsford was a record breaker, achieving 13 scores of over 200 in his career and 2 scores of over 400 with his highest innings being a lengthy 437 for Victoria versus Queensland at the Melbourne Cricket Ground in 1927/28. He was unsuccessful on two of his three visits to England in 1926 he suffered with tonsillitis, in 1930 he achieved 1,425 runs (av. 49.13) and in 1934 he showed the English public what they had missed on his previous two tours when he scored 1,784 runs (av. 77.56). He was awarded an MBE for his services to the game and he died at Kyneton, Victoria in 1991.

Born in Dunedin, New Zealand in 1891, Clarence 'Clarrie' Grimmett was a lower order right-handed batsman and brilliant leg-break and googly bowler. He played 5 matches for Victoria from 1918/19 to 1923/24 and later joined South Australia for whom he played 105 matches between 1924/25 and 1940/41. Grimmett toured England in 1926, 1930 and 1934. He played 13 of his 37 Tests for Australia on English soil, scoring 217 runs (av. 14.47) with a top score of 50 at Old Trafford in 1930. He bagged 67 wickets (av. 29.96), with a best haul of 6 for 167 at Lord's in 1930 and he held 5 catches. He took 100 wickets on each of his three tours of England, with a best of 144 wickets (av. 16.85) in 1930. Playing against Yorkshire at Bramall Lane, Sheffield in 1930, he took all 10 wickets for just 37 runs in an innings. He was the first Test bowler to take over 200 wickets in a Test career and he died in the Kensington Park district of Adelaide in 1980.

The rival captains, Percy Chapman of England *(left)* and Bill Woodfull of Australia *(right)*, look at the coin as it falls to the ground during the toss for the First Test match at Trent Bridge in 1930.

The Australians take to the field for the First Test of the 1930 series at Trent Bridge. From left to right: Tim Wall, Bill Woodfull, Vic Richardson, Bert Oldfield, Alan Fairfax, Don Bradman, Clarrie Grimmett, Stan McCabe, P.M. Hornibrook, Alan Kippax. Bill Ponsford is obscured behind Alan Fairfax.

The First Test match of the series at Trent Bridge in 1930, viewed from the Pavilion looking towards the Radcliffe Road End of the ground. Australian opening batsman Bill Ponsford has just faced a menacing delivery from England's Maurice Tate.

The First Test in progress at Trent Bridge, viewed from the Member's Pavilion looking towards the Radcliffe Road End, with the city of Nottingham beyond. Alan Fairfax is bowling to England's Herbert Sutcliffe.

Bill Ponsford is bowled by Maurice Tate during Australia's first innings at Trent Bridge in 1930. George Duckworth, the wicketkeeper, has caught a flying stump.

Jack Hobbs is in to bat during his fine innings for England in the first innings of the First Test match at Trent Bridge. Hobbs played his part manfully whilst other wickets fell around him between the showers.

England's Walter Robins batting in the First Test match at Trent Bridge.

Vic Richardson is bowled by Ernest Tyldesley during Australia's first innings at Trent Bridge.

Alan Fairfax bowling at Trent Bridge during England's second innings in 1930. Herbert Sutcliffe is the England batsman looking on.

The crowd at Trent Bridge surrounds Percy Chapman as he leads the England team off the field after they have beaten Australia by 97 runs in a game that was full of incidents.

The two captains, Bill Woodfull of Australia and Percy Chapman of England, inspect the wicket at Old Trafford on the morning of the first day of the Fourth Test match of the series in 1930.

Australian opening batsmen Bill Woodfull and Bill Ponsford come out from the Old Trafford Pavilion to open the innings for Australia in the Fourth Test with England at Manchester in 1930.

A characteristic stroke to leg by England's Jack Hobbs during the second day of the Test match at Old Trafford in 1930. The Australian close fielder is Clarrie Grimmett and the wicketkeeper is Bertie Oldfield.

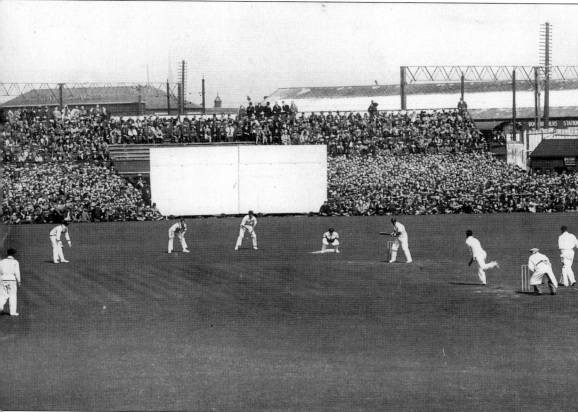

Tim Wall, Australia's quick bowler, bowls to Duleepsinhji at Old Trafford in 1930. The Manchester to Altrincham railway line gantries can be seen in the background.

Bill Ponsford in action during his first wicket partnership with Bill Woodfull in the Fourth Test match of the 1930 series at Old Trafford.

The England wicketkeeper, George Duckworth, desperate to break the Australian opening partnership at Old Trafford, falls while trying to run out Bill Ponsford.

Don Bradman, the legendary Australian batsman, is dismissed, caught in the gully by Duleepsinhji. The Old Trafford spectators experienced mixed feelings of regret and triumph when Bradman lost his wicket during the Fourth Test match at Manchester in 1930.

Clarrie Grimmett makes a big hit during his fine innings for Australia in the Fourth Test match at Old Trafford in 1930.

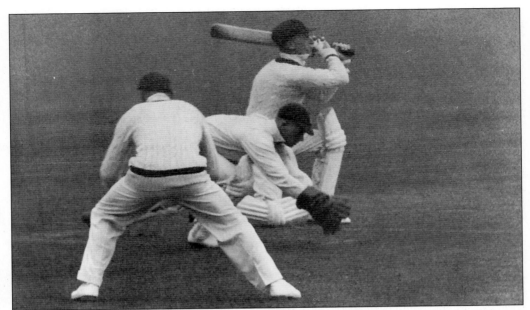

Clarrie Grimmett is seen batting at Old Trafford during the Fourth Test match of the series in 1930.

The Old Trafford Cricket Ground in 1930 during the Fourth Test match of the series. The photograph was taken at the Stretford End, looking towards the Warwick Road End of the ground

Above left: Ian Peebles of Middlesex bowls to Alan Fairfax of Australia at Old Trafford during the Test match in 1930. England wicketkeeper George Duckworth looks on. *Above right:* Australian batsman Bill Ponsford has just offered a difficult chance to England skipper Percy Chapman at Old Trafford during the 1930 Test match.

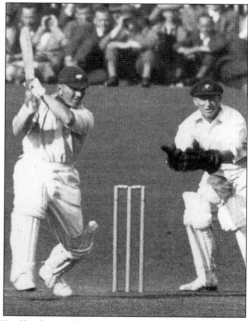

Above left: A section of the huge crowd at Old Trafford watch the Fourth Test match of the 1930 series between England and Australia. *Above right:* Yorkshire's Maurice Leyland drives Stan McCabe to the boundary during the Fourth Test at Old Trafford in 1930. Bertie Oldfield, the Australian wicketkeeper, watches the action from behind the stumps.

A general view of the scene at Kennington Oval during the Fifth Test of the series, when Bill Woodfull and Bill Ponsford were getting Australia off to a good start in 1930.

Herbert Sutcliffe is hurt by a ball from Peter Hornibrook when he was standing firm for England, during his great effort at Kennington Oval in 1930.

Wally Hammond misses one from Clarrie Grimmett at Kennington Oval. The slow bowler has brought in his fielder to snap up any chance offering off the tricky wicket.

The relief of the Englishmen when George Duckworth caught Bill Woodfull at Kennington Oval in 1930.

A sensational incident during the Fifth Test of the 1930 Test series at Kennington Oval. Herbert Sutcliffe, just scrapes home in answering a call for a close one from Jack Hobbs, who is seen watching over his shoulder while he runs. Had the Australian fielder been a little more accurate in his throw-in, this might well have struck disaster for England.

Stubborn Australian opener Bill Ponsford plays Ian Peebles at Kennington Oval during the Fifth Test of the 1930 series, watched by wicketkeeper George Duckworth.

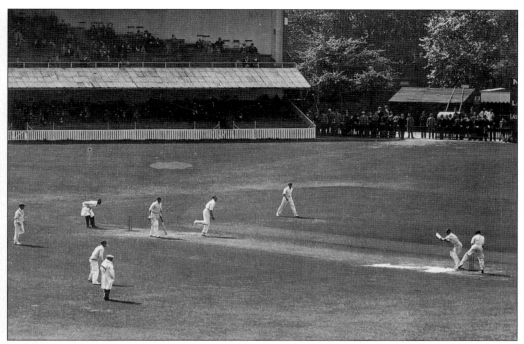

The scene at the Kennington Oval in 1930 when England, after a blank day owing to rain, resumed their second innings task against Australia. Herbert Sutcliffe faces Alan Fairfax with Walter Whysall the non striking batsman.

Archie Jackson plays a ball from Maurice Tate during his stand with Don Bradman at Kennington Oval in 1930.

Australian middle-order batsman Archie Jackson, on his only tour of England, drives against England in the Fifth Test of the 1930 series at Kennington Oval, watched by George Duckworth behind the stumps and an England close fielder.

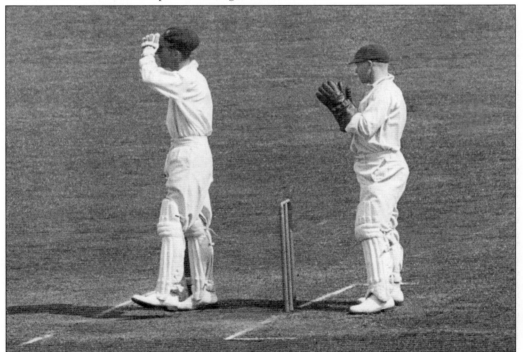

Archie Jackson acknowledges the cheers of the Kennington Oval crowd and England wicketkeeper George Duckworth on reaching his 50.

Don Bradman, the wonder batsman, acknowledges the cheers of the Kennington Oval crowd after scoring yet another century in 1930.

Crowds enjoy glorious weather for the marathon Fifth Test of the 1930 series at Kennington Oval. Play is taking place in the shadows of the famous gasholders which are synonymous with the ground.

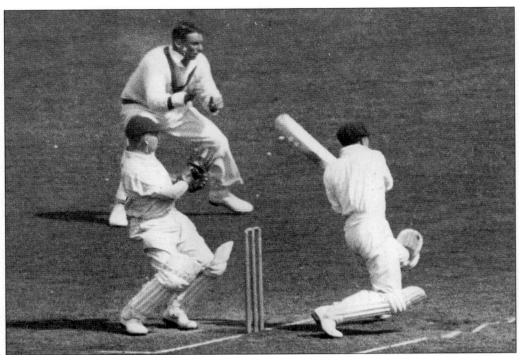

Don Bradman hits out during his partnership with Archie Jackson at the Kennington Oval in 1930.

Herbert Sutcliffe cuts Clarrie Grimmett for two. This took place during the continuation of his great innings of 161 at Kennington Oval in the Fifth Test of the series.

Don Bradman hammers sawdust into the rain-soaked pitch when the game was resumed at Kennington Oval in 1930.

England commence their second innings task with Herbert Sutcliffe playing Alan Fairfax at Kennington Oval in 1930 as Bertie Oldfield looks on.

Don Bradman acknowledges the cheers of the Kennington Oval crowd on reaching 200 in 1930. Jack Hobbs and George Duckworth are seen applauding.

Don Bradman plays a delivery from Wally Hammond. Archie Jackson is the non-striking batsman.

Wicketkeeper Bertie Oldfield and close fielder Tim Wall look on as Maurice Leyland is bowled by Peter Hornibrook in England's second innings at the Kennington Oval. Shortly afterwards, England had been beaten by an innings and 39 runs, consequently losing the Ashes in 1930.

Australia wins the Ashes at Kennington Oval in 1930. Bob Wyatt is bowled by Peter Hornibrook towards the end of the England second innings in 1930.

Above left: Alan Kippax makes a characteristic stroke during the Australian first innings at Kennington Oval in 1930. *Above right*: Herbert Sutcliffe hits a ball from Peter Hornibrook to the boundary during his fighting innings at Kennington Oval in 1930.

The huge crowd rush onto the field after play ended at Kennington Oval in 1930 when Australia had won the Ashes.

The teams appear on the balcony at the end of the series in 1930 after Australia had won the Ashes. Young Don Bradman is in the centre of the balcony.

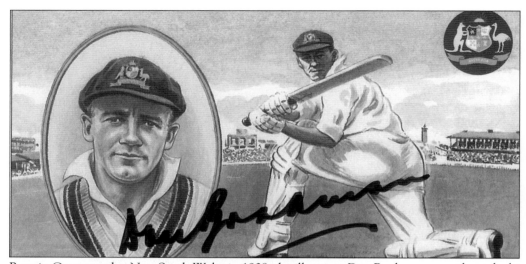

Born in Cootamundra, New South Wales in 1908, the illustrious Don Bradman was without doubt the greatest of all Test cricketers to grace these shores. An outstanding right-handed middle order batsman and occasional leg-break bowler, he toured with Australia to England in 1930, 1934, 1938 and 1948. Whilst in England Bradman played 19 of his 52 Tests, scoring a mammoth 2,674 runs (av. 102.85), with a highest innings of 334 at Headingley in 1930. He also held 5 catches and his best bowling performance was 0 for 1 at Lord's in 1930. Other than his highest score of 334 at Headingley, Bradman accumulated many runs during each of his four tours of England. In 1930 he recorded Test centuries against England at three different grounds – 131 at Trent Bridge, 232 at Kennington Oval and 254 at Lord's, which he regarded as his best innings on English soil. Four years later he scored 304 in Tests at Headingley and 244 at Kennington Oval. This was followed in 1938 with 3 Test match hundreds – 144 not out at Trent Bridge, 102 not out at Lord's and 103 at Headingley. In 1948, in his final Test series in England, he reached 138 at Trent Bridge and 173 not out at Headingley. A truly magnificent batsman, the crowds flocked to all Test and county cricket grounds around the country whenever the great man was batting for the touring Australians. His highest individual innings was 452 not out, which he made for New South Wales versus Queensland at the Sydney Cricket Ground in 1929/30. He played 41 matches for New South Wales between 1927/28 and 1933/34 and later represented South Australia in 44 matches from 1935/36 to 1948/49. His achievements at the wicket in England in first-class matches were second to none. In 1930 he amassed 2,960 runs (av. 98.66), with 10 hundreds; in 1934 he scored 2,020 runs (av. 84.16), with 7 hundreds; in 1938 he scored 2,429 runs (av. 115.66) with 13 hundreds; in 1948 he amassed 2,428 runs (av. 89.92) with 11 hundreds. He was knighted for his services to cricket and he died on 25 February 2001.

Born in Sydney in 1897, Alan Kippax was a stylish right-handed middle order batsman and leg-break bowler. He played 87 games for New South Wales between 1918/19 and 1935/36 and toured England in 1930 and 1934. He played 6 of his 22 Tests in England, scoring 365 runs (av. 45.63) with a highest score of 83 at Lord's in 1930, and he held 5 catches. His most successful tour was in 1930 when he amassed 1,451 runs (av. 58.04). His highest individual innings was his triple hundred 315 not out for New South Wales versus Queensland at Sydney Cricket Ground in 1927/28. He died in the Bellevue district of Sydney in 1972.

Born in Lanark, Scotland in 1909, Archie Jackson was a superb right-handed middle order batsman and good slip fielder. He represented New South Wales 28 times between 1926/27 and 1930/31 and toured England with Australia in 1930. He played 2 of his 8 Tests in England, scoring 74 runs (av. 37.00), with a top score of 73 at Kennington Oval in 1930, and holding a single catch. During this tour he amassed 1,097 runs (av. 34.28), but failed to live up to the reputation he had brought with him from down under. Tragically, he died of tuberculosis in Brisbane, Queensland in 1933.

Stan McCabe was born in Grenfell, New South Wales in 1910. He was an excellent right-handed middle order batsman and right-arm medium pace bowler who represented New South Wales 55 times between 1928/29 and 1941/42. McCabe toured England in 1930, 1934 and 1938. A forceful batsman, he amassed 1,055 runs (av. 47.95) in 14 of his 39 Tests in England, with a highest innings of 232 at Trent Bridge. He also took 14 wickets (av. 52.36) with a best performance of 4 for 41 and he held 13 catches. His best tour was in 1934 when he amassed 2,078 runs (av. 69.26) with a highest innings of 240 for the tourists against Surrey at Kennington Oval. He died in the Mosman district of Sydney in 1968.

Tim Wall was born in Adelaide in 1904. A right-arm fast bowler, right-handed tail-end batsman and good short leg fielder, he toured England in 1930 and 1938, He played 9 of his 18 Tests for Australia on English soil, scoring 32 runs (av. 4.57). He had a top score of 18 at Old Trafford in 1934 and bagged 19 wickets (av. 56.05) with a best performance of 4 for 108 at Lord's in 1934. During the 1930 tour his electric pace saw him take 56 Test wickets (av. 29.25) and in Tests in 1934 he bagged 42 wickets (av. 30.71). He died in Adelaide in 1981.

The team of 1930. From left to right, back row: W.L. Kelly (manager), A. Jackson, T.W. Wall, E.L. a'Beckett, P.M. Hornibrook, A. Hurwood, C.V. Grimmett, T. Howard (treasurer). Middle row: A.G. Fairfax, W.H. Ponsford, V.Y. Richardson (vice-captain), W.M. Woodfull (captain), A.F. Kippax, D.G. Bradman, C.W. Walker. Front row: S.J. McCabe, W.A.S. Oldfield. The 1930 Australian side played 31 first-class matches, winning 11, losing 1 and drawing 18 matches with one match tied. They also played 3 second-class matches with 1 win, 1 draw and 1 abandoned game. The Test match series saw a 5-Test rubber with 2 wins, 1 loss and 2 drawn Tests.

The Australian touring team of 1930 ahead of their match versus Mr H.D.G. Leveson-Gower's XI which was staged at the Scarborough Cricket Festival, North Marine Drive, Scarborough between 10 and 12 September 1930. From left to right: A.F. Kippax, W.A.S.Oldfield, C.V. Grimmett, S.J. McCabe, A. Jackson, T.W. Wall, A. Hurwood, V.Y. Richardson (captain), P.M. Hornibrook, A.G. Fairfax, D.G. Bradman.

A print of a poster from the Third Test match between England and Australia at Headingley in 1930.

Don Bradman takes to the field at North Marine Road, Scarborough during the Festival match in 1930.

Four

Bradman Tours 1934 to 1948

The Australians in 1934. From left to right, back row: W. Ferguson (scorer), W.A. Brown, E.H. Bromley, T.W. Wall, H. Bushby (manager), W.J. O'Reilly, L. O'B. Fleetwood-Smith, L.S. Darling, C.V. Grimmett, W.C. Bull (treasurer). Middle row: H.I. Ebeling, A.G. Chipperfield, D.G. Bradman (vice-captain), W.M. Woodfull (captain), A.F. Kippax, S.J. McCabe, W.A.S. Oldfield. Front row: B.A. Barnett, W.H. Ponsford. The 1934 Australian side played 30 first-class matches, winning 13, losing 1 and drawing 16. They also played 4 second-class matches with 2 wins and 2 drawn fixtures. The Test Match Series saw a 5-Test rubber with 2 won, 1 loss and 2 drawn Tests.

ENGLAND v. AUSTRALIA, at Headingley.

ENGLAND. 1st Innings — 2nd Innings

1. C. F. Walters c and b Chipperfield 44 — *b* O'REILLY 45
2. Keeton c Oldfield b O'Reilly 25 — ..*b* GRIMMETT 12
3. Hammond b Wall 37 — RUN OUT 20
4. Hendren b Chipperfield 29 — *lbw* O'REILLY 42
5. R. E. S. Wyatt c Oldfield b Grimmett 19 — *b* GRIMMETT 44
6. Leyland lbw b O'Reilly 16 — NOT OUT 49
7. Ames b Grimmett 9 — c BROWN b GRIMMETT 8
8. Hopwood lbw b O'Reilly 8 — NOT OUT 2
9. Verity not out 4
10. Mitchell (T. B.) st Oldfield b Grimmett 9
11. Bowes c Ponsford b Grimmett 0
Extras lb, 2. 2 — Extras 7

Total 200 — Total for 6 wkts 229

Total runs at fall of each wicket
43 85 135 168 170 189 189 200 200

Bowler	Overs	Maidens	Runs	W'kts	Overs	Maidens	Runs	W'kts
Wall	18	1	57	1	14	5	36	0
McCabe	4	2	3	0	4	5	5	0
Grimmett	30·4	11	57	4	56·5	24	72	3
O'Reilly	35	16	46	3	51	25	88	2
Chipperfield	18	6	35	2	9	2	21	0

Umpires:
Messrs. Hardstaff & Dolphin

Scorers:
Messrs. Ringrose & Ferguson

AUSTRALIA. 1st Innings — 2nd Innings

1. W. Brown b Bowes 15
2. W. H. Ponsford not out hit wkt b Bowes 181 186
3. D. G. Bradman b Bowes 304
4. S. McCabe b Bowes 27
5. W. M. Woodfull b Bowes 0
6. L. Darling b Bowes 12
7. A. G. Chipperfield c Wyatt b Verity 1
8. W. Oldfield c Ames b Bowes 0
9. C. V. Grimmett RUN OUT 15
10. W. J. O'Reilly NOT OUT 11
11. T. Wall lbw b Verity 1
Extras 17 — Extras

Total for 8 wkts 584 — Total

Total runs at fall of each wicket
37·39·39· 427· 517· 550· 551· 557· 574·584

Bowler	Overs	Maidens	Runs	W'kts	Overs	Maidens	Runs	W'kts
BOWES	50.	13	142	6				
HAMMOND	29.	5	82	0				
MITCHELL	23	1	117	0				
VERITY	46·5	15	113	3				
HOPWOOD	30	7	93	0				
LEYLAND	6	0	20	0				

HOURS OF PLAY—1st day, 11·30 to 6·30; other days, 11·0 to 6·30.
Luncheon Interval, 1·30 to 2·15 each day. Tea, 4·30.

A partly completed scorecard of the England versus Australia Test match at Headingley on 20 to 24 July 1934. Don Bradman scored 304 of Australia's 1st innings total of 584 all-out.

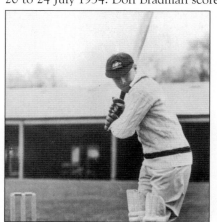 

Left: Born in Sydney in 1905, Arthur Chipperfield was a right-handed middle order batsman, leg break bowler and excellent slip fielder. He played 30 matches for New South Wales between 1933/34 and 1939/40 and also played 6 of his 14 Tests for Australia in England in 1934 and 1938. Chipperfield scored 201 runs (av. 25.13), with a highest score of 99 at Trent Bridge and he recorded a best bowling performance of 3 for 91 at Headingley in 1934 and he took 8 catches. He died in the Ryde district of Sydney in 1987. *Right:* Born in Toowoomba, Queensland in 1912, William 'Bill' Brown was a right-handed opening batsman, off-break bowler and excellent fielder. He represented New South Wales in 22 matches from 1932/33 to 1934/35 and also played for Queensland in 50 matches from 1936/37 to 1949/50. He toured England in 1934, 1938 and 1948 and he played a total of 11 of his 22 Tests for Australia in England. He scored 885 runs (av. 46.58), with a best performance of 206 not out at Lord's in 1938, and he also held 7 catches. He scored 1,000 runs on each of his tours of England, with a best performance of 1,854 runs (av. 57.93). His highest individual innings in England was his 265 not out for the Australians versus Derbyshire at Queen's Park, Chesterfield in 1938.

Born in White Cliffs, New South Wales in 1905, Bill O'Reilly was a lower order left-handed batsman and leg break and googly bowler. He represented New South Wales 54 times between 1927/28 to 1945/46 and he toured with Australia to England in 1934 and 1938. He played in 9 of his 27 Tests in England, taking 50 wickets (av. 26.16) with a best performance of 7 for 54 at Trent Bridge in 1934. He scored 160 runs (av. 20.00) with a top score of 42 at Lord's in 1938 and he held 2 catches. His best tour of England was in 1934, when he topped the tour averages with 109 wickets (av. 17.04) and also the Test averages with 28 wickets (av. 24.92). In 1938 he bagged 104 wickets (av. 16.59) in first-class games and 22 wickets (av. 27.72) in Tests. His best bowling performance in England was his 9 for 38 for the tourists against Somerset at Taunton in 1934. He died in the Sutherland district of Sydney in 1992.

Born in Stawell, Victoria in 1908, Leslie Fleetwood-Smith was a right-handed lower order batsman and slow left-arm bowler with chinamen. He represented Victoria from 1931/32 to 1939/40 in 51 matches and toured England in 1934 and 1938. He played 4 of his 10 Tests for Australia in England and bagged 14 wickets (av. 51.93), with best figures of 4 for 34 at Headingley in 1938. He scored 30 runs (av. 15.00), with a highest score of 16 not out at Kennington Oval in 1938. In 1934 he bagged 106 wickets (av. 19.20), and he performed well as a partnering bowler with Bill O'Reilly. He died in Fitzroy district of Melbourne in 1971.

The 1938 Australians. From left to right, back row: W.H. Jeanes (manager), S.G. Barnes, E.L. McCormick, W.J. O'Reilly, E.C.S. White, L. O'B. Fleetwood-Smith, J.H. Fingleton, W. Ferguson (scorer). Middle row: W.A. Brown, A.G. Chipperfield, S.J. McCabe (vice-captain), D.G. Bradman (captain), B.A. Barnett, M.G. Waite and F.A. Ward. Front row: C.W. Walker, C.L. Badcock, A.L. Hassett. The 1938 Australian side played 30 first-class matches, winning 15, losing 2 and drawing 12, with a single match abandoned due to poor weather. They also played 6 second-class matches with 5 wins and 1 drawn game. The Test match series saw a 5-Test rubber with 1 Test match won, 1 lost, 1 abandoned and 2 drawn.

Born in Geelong, Victoria in 1913, Lindsay Hassett was a right-handed middle order batsman and right-arm medium pace bowler. He played 73 games for his native Victoria between 1932/33 and 1952/53, which included his career best score of 232 for Victoria versus the touring MCC at Melbourne Cricket Ground in 1950/51. Hassett toured England in 1938, 1948 and 1953. He played 14 of his 43 Tests whilst in England, scoring 874 runs (av. 34.96), with a highest score of 137 at Trent Bridge in 1948. His best bowling was 0 for 4 at Kennington Oval in 1953 and he held 9 catches. He achieved 1,000 runs on each of his tours of England, with a best performance of 1,589 (av. 54.79) in 1938 and 1,563 (av. 74.42) in 1948. He was awarded an MBE for his services to cricket and died in 1993.

Above left: Lindsay Badcock was born in Exton, Tasmania in 1914 and he toured England in 1938. He played 4 of his 7 Tests whilst in England, scoring 32 runs (av. 4.57), with a top score of 9 at Trent Bridge and also at Kennington Oval. A right-handed top order batsman who took on the bowlers, he played 19 games for his native Tasmania between 1929/30 and 1933/34. He amassed 1,604 runs (av. 45.82) whilst touring England in 1938. Sadly, he had to retire from the game at the age of twenty-seven as he suffered from lumbago. He died in Exton, Tasmania in 1982. *Above right:* Born in Charters Towers, Queensland in 1916, Sid Barnes was a right-handed opening batsman and leg-break bowler. He played 56 matches for New South Wales between 1936/37 and 1952/53 and he toured England twice in 1938 and 1948. He played 5 of his 13 Tests for Australia in England, scoring 403 runs (av. 67.17), and had a highest innings of 141 at Lord's in 1948. He took 1 wicket (av. 95.00) with a best of 1 for 84 at Kennington Oval in 1938 and he held 2 catches. His best tour of England was in 1948 when he scored 1,354 runs (av. 56.81). His career ended after he had criticised the Australian Cricket Authorities through the press. He died in Collaroy district of Sydney in 1973.

'Jack' Fingleton was born in the Waverley suburb of Sydney in 1908 and, as a right-handed opening batsman and sound fielder, he represented New South Wales in 49 matches between 1928/29 and 1939/40. Fingleton toured England in 1938 and he played in 4 of his 18 Tests in England scoring 123 runs (av. 20.50) and holding 2 catches. His highest score of 40 was recorded at Trent Bridge. His best tour was in 1938 when he amassed 1,141 runs (av. 38.03). After retiring from the game he became a well-known cricket writer on the game and he wrote several major books about the sport. He died in the St Leonards district of Sydney in 1981.

The 'Invincibles', the Australians of 1948. From left to right, back row: R.N. Harvey, S.G. Barnes, R.R. Lindwall, R.A. Saggers, D.T. Ring, W.A. Johnston, E.R.H. Toshack, K.R. Miller, D. Tallon, S.J.E. Loxton. Front row: K. Johnson (manager), R.A. Hammence, I.W. Johnson, A.L. Hassett, D.G. Bradman (captain), W.A. Brown, A.R. Morris, C.L. McCool, W. Ferguson (scorer). The 1948 Australian side, led by Don Bradman on his last tour of England, played 31 first-class matches winning 23, losing 0 and drawing 8. They also played 3 second-class matches with 2 wins and 1 draw. The Test match series saw a 5-Test rubber with 4 Test wins and 1 defeat.

Above left: A Committee Stand ticket for the Australians' opening tour match at New Road, Worcester against Worcestershire on 29 April 1948. *Above right:* A ticket for the England versus Australia Test match at Headingley on 22 July 1948.

Born in Bondi, Sydney in 1922, Arthur Morris was a left-handed opening batsman and left-arm slow bowler. He played 50 matches for New South Wales between 1940/41 and 1954/55 and he toured England in 1948 and 1953. He played in 10 of his 46 Tests for Australia in England, scoring 1,033 runs (av. 57.39), with a highest score of 196 at Kennington Oval in 1948. He took 1 wicket (av. 39.00) with a best performance of 1 for 5 at Old Trafford in 1953 and he held 6 catches. His first tour of England was also his best – he accumulated 1,922 runs (av. 71.18), with a top score of 290 for the tourists against Gloucestershire at Bristol and he also topped the Test batting averages with 696 runs (av. 87.00). He was awarded an MBE for his services to cricket.

Neil Harvey was born in the Fitzroy district of Melbourne in 1928. He initially played for Victoria in 64 matches between 1946/47 and 1956/57 as a left-handed middle order batsman, off-break bowler and exceptional fielder. He later joined New South Wales in 1958/59 and played 30 matches for them until 1962/63. Harvey toured England in 1948, 1953, 1956 and 1961. He played 17 of his 79 Tests whilst in England, scoring 1,014 runs (av. 33.80), with a highest score of 122 at Old Trafford in 1953. His best bowling was 0 for 0 at Kennington Oval in 1961 and he held 5 catches. He scored over 1,000 runs on each of his tours of England with a best performance of 2,040 runs (av. 65.80) in 1953. He was awarded an MBE for his services to the game.

Above left: Born in Sunshine, Melbourne in 1919, Keith Miller was an attacking right-handed middle order batsman and right-arm fast bowler. He represented Victoria 18 times from 1937/38 to 1946/47, New South Wales 50 times from 1947/48 to 1955/56 and Nottinghamshire in only a single game in 1959. Miller represented Australia in 15 of his 55 Tests whilst in England and he toured England in 1948, 1953 and 1956. He scored 610 runs (av. 24.40), achieved 44 wickets (av. 24.34) and he took 13 catches. His best performances were 109 with the bat at Lord's in 1953 and 5 for 72 and 5 for 80 in the same Test at Lord's in 1956. His best tour of England was in 1953, when he scored 1,433 runs (av. 51.17) and his highest score was 281 not out for the tourists versus Leicestershire at Grace Road, Leicester in 1956. Having retired from the game, Miller became a respected and forthright cricket writer and journalist. *Above right:* William 'Bill' Johnston was born in Beeac, Victoria in 1922. A left-handed lower order batsman and left-arm fast medium or slow spin bowler, he played 56 games for Victoria from 1945/46 to 1954/55. He played 8 of his 40 Tests in England for Australia during his two tours in 1948 and 1953. He scored 84 runs (av. 28.00), bagged 34 wickets (av. 28.62) and he held 2 catches. His best performances were 29 at Lord's in 1948 and 5 for 36 at Trent Bridge in 1948. His most successful tour to England was his first, in 1948, when he achieved 102 wickets (av. 16.42).

Born in Bundaberg, Queensland in 1916, Don Tallon was a wicketkeeper and lower order right-handed batsman. He toured England in 1948 and 1953, during which time he played 5 of his 21 Tests for Australia in England, scoring 127 runs (av. 21.17) with a highest innings of 53 at Lord's in 1948. He played 86 games for Queensland between 1933/34 and 1953/54. Don Tallon died in Bundaberg, Queensland in 1984.

Born in Mascot, Sydney in 1921, Ray Lindwall was a right-handed lower order hard hitting batsman and excellent right-arm fast medium bowler. He represented New South Wales in 50 matches and Queensland in 34 matches together between 1941/42 and 1959/60 and he toured England in 1948, 1953 and 1956. He played 14 of his 61 Tests for Australia in England, scoring 386 runs (av. 22.71), bagged 60 wickets (av. 20.97) and he took 7 catches. His best batting and bowling performances were 77 at Headingley in 1948 and 6 for 20 at Kennington Oval in 1948. His best tour of England was 1948, when he bagged 86 wickets (av. 15.68). He was awarded an MBE for his services to the game of cricket.

The 20th Australian tourists of 1948 at New Road, Worcester ahead of the opening tour fixture with Worcestershire on 28 April 1948. From left to right, back row: I.W. Johnson, A.R. Morris, E.L. Toshack, K.R. Miller, D. Tallon, R.R. Lindwall, R.N. Harvey. Front row: W.A. Brown, A.L. Hassett, D.G. Bradman (captain), C.L. McCool, S.G. Barnes.

The Australians of 1948 at Scarborough in front of the Pavilion before their match with Mr H.D.G. Leveson-Gower's XI, which took place at North Marine Road between 8 and 10 September 1948. H.D.G. Leveson-Gower's XI 177 (R.R. Lindwall 6 for 59) and 75 for 2 drew with the Australians 489 for 8 declared (D.G. Bradman 153, S.G. Barnes 151, A.R. Morris 62).

Left: Gubby Allen of Middlesex and England *(left)* with Don Bradman of Australia *(right)*, pictured at Lord's in 1948. *Right:* Arthur Morris *(left)* and Sidney Barnes *(right)* take to the field at the Scarborough Cricket Festival in 1948.

Five

Fifties and Sixties 1953 to 1968

The Australians of 1953. From left to right, back row: R.R. Lindwall, A.K. Davidson, D.T. Ring, J.C. Hill, G.R.A. Langley. Middle row: G.B. Hole, R.G. Archer, W.A. Johnston, K.R. Miller, R. Benaud, D. Tallon. Front row: I.D. Craig, J.H. de Courcy, A.L. Hassett (captain), G.A. Davies (manager), A.R. Morris (vice-captain), R.N. Harvey, C.C. McDonald. The 1953 Australian side played 33 first-class matches, winning 16, losing 1 and drawing 16. They also played 2 second-class matches, drawing both. The Test match series saw a 5-Test rubber with 1 Test lost and 4 drawn.

Above left: Touring England with Australia in 1953, 1956 and 1961, Alan Davidson played in 12 Tests. He bagged 33 wickets (av. 25.45), scored 341 runs (av. 24.36) and he held 11 catches. His best batting and bowling performances were both recorded during the 1961 series: 77 not out at Old Trafford and 5 for 42 at Lord's. *Above right:* Born in Penrith, New South Wales in 1930, Richie Benaud was a right-handed forceful middle order batsman and splendid leg-break and googly bowler. He played 86 games for his native New South Wales from 1948/49 to 1963/64 and he toured England in 1953, 1956 and 1961. He played 12 of his 63 Tests for Australia in England, scoring 260 runs (av. 14.44) with a top score of 97 at Lord's in 1956. As a bowler, he bagged 25 wickets av. 39.68), with a best haul of 6 for 70 at Old Trafford in 1961, and he held 12 catches. He captained the team in England in 1961 and led the tourists to victory, even though he suffered an injury which reduced his bowling ability. After retiring from the game he became a leading cricket journalist, writer and broadcaster all around the cricket world. He was awarded an OBE for his services to the game of cricket.

Born in Yass, New South Wales in 1935, Ian Craig was a right-handed middle order batsman, slow right-arm bowler and good deep fielder. He represented New South Wales between 1951/52 and 1961/62 in 55 matches and he toured England in 1953 and 1956. He played only 2 of his 11 Tests in England when, aged 17 years, he scored 55 runs (av. 13.75), with a highest innings of 38 at Old Trafford in 1956. His career-best innings was his 213 not out for New South Wales versus the touring South Africans at the Sydney Cricket Ground in 1952/53.

Lindsay Hassett (*left*) and Alan Davidson (*right*) walk towards the wicket at Scarborough during the cricket festival match in 1953.

The 22nd Australian tourists in England 1956. From left to right, back row: J.W. Burke, K.D. Mackay, I.D. Craig, P.J.P. Burge, R. Benaud, W.P.A. Crawford, R.G. Archer, J.W. Rutherford, J.W. Wilson. Front row: L.V. Maddocks, C.C. McDonald, K.R. Miller, I.W. Johnson (captain), R.R. Lindwall, G.R.A. Langley, R.N. Harvey, A.K. Davidson. The 1956 Australian side played 31 first-class matches, winning 9, losing 3 and drawing 19. They also played 4 second-class matches with 2 wins, 1 draw and 1 abandoned game. The Test match series saw a 5-Test rubber with 1 win, 2 loss and 2 drawn Tests.

'From First over - To Close of Play Daily Express for full sports coverage' advertising card depicting the 1956 Australian touring side.

Above left: Ken 'Slasher' Mackay was born in Windsor, Queensland in 1925. He was a stubborn left-handed batsman and right-arm medium pace bowler who represented Queensland from 1946/47 to 1963/64 109 times. He toured England in 1956 and 1961 and played 8 of his 37 Tests for Australia in England, during which time he accumulated 231 runs (av. 17.77), with a highest score of 64 at Edgbaston in 1961. He also took 17 wickets (av. 33.47) with a best haul of 5 for 121 at Kennington Oval in 1961 and he held 4 catches. His best tour to England was in 1956, when he scored 1,103 runs (av. 52.52). He died at Stradbroke Island, Queensland in 1982. *Above right:* Born in Mosman, Sydney in 1930, Jim Burke was a right-handed opening batsman and off-break bowler who played 67 matches for New South Wales between 1948/49 and 1958/59. He toured England in 1956 and played in all 5 Tests during the summer, scoring 271 runs (av. 30.11) with a top score of 65 at Lord's. His best bowling performance was 0 for 6 at Trent Bridge. His best tour of England was in 1956, when he amassed 1,339 runs (av. 47.82). Having retired from the game he became a well-respected sports commentator. He died in Manly, Sydney in 1979.

Born at Kangaroo Point, Brisbane in 1932, Peter Burge played 91 matches for his native Queensland between 1952/53 and 1967/68. He toured England with Australia in 1956, 1961 and 1964. He played 13 of his 42 Tests whilst in England with Australia, scoring 738 runs (av. 38.84), with a highest score of 181 at Kennington Oval in 1961, and he held 5 catches. He hit 1,000 runs in two of his three tours to England, with a best of 1,376 runs (av. 55.04) in 1961. His career-best score was his 283 for Queensland versus New South Wales at the 'Gabba' Brisbane in 1963/64. Since retiring from the game he has served the I.C.C. as an international match referee.

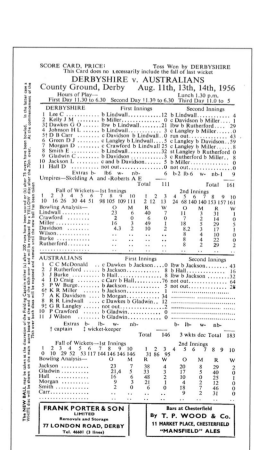

A copy of the completed scorecard from the Derbyshire versus Australians match at the County Cricket Ground, Derby on 11, 13 and 14 August 1956 when the Australians won by 57 runs.

The Australian cricket team 1961. From left to right, back row: B.C. Booth, W.M. Lawry, F.M. Mission, R.A. Gaunt, G.D. McKenzie. Middle row: A. James (physiotherapist), J. Cameron (scorer), B.N. Jarman, I.W. Quick, R.C. Steele (treasurer), L.F. Kline, N.C. O'Neill, P.J.P. Burge, R.B. Simpson. Front row, left to right: A.T.W. Grout, A.K. Davidson, R. Benaud (captain), S.G. Webb (manager), R.N. Harvey, C.C. McDonald, K.D. Mackay. The 1961 Australian side played 32 first-class matches, winning 13, losing 1 and drawing 18 matches. They also played 4 second-class matches with 2 wins, 1 draw and 1 abandoned match. The Test match series saw a 5-Test rubber with 2 wins, 1 loss and 2 drawn Tests.

Born in Melbourne in 1937, the opening batsman William 'Bill' Lawry toured England with Australia in 1961, 1964 and 1968. He played in 14 of his 67 Tests in England, amassing 1,007 runs (av. 45.77) with a top score of 135 at Kennington Oval in 1968, and he held 7 catches. Lawry was a sound left-handed top order batsman and left-arm medium pace bowler who played 99 matches for Victoria from 1955/56 to 1970/71. His best tour of England was in 1961 when he topped both the Tour and Test batting averages. During the tour he scored 2,019 runs (av. 61.18) and in Tests that summer he amassed 420 runs (av. 52.50). Lawry captained Australia in 25 of his 67 Tests, 9 of which he captained against England. His career-best score was 266 for Victoria versus New South Wales at the Sydney Cricket Ground in 1960/61. Since retiring from the game he has served the game as a respected television and radio commentator for both Channel 9 and the Australian Broadcasting Corporation.

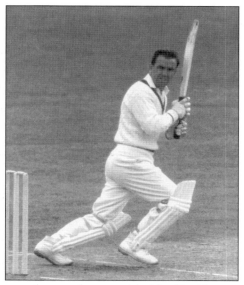

Above left: Born in Perth in 1941, Graham McKenzie, seen here at the nets with Alan Davidson at Lord's, was a right-arm fast-medium bowler and late order right-handed batsman. He represented Western Australia in 81 matches from 1959/60 to 1973/74, Leicestershire in 151 matches between 1969 and 1975 and Transvaal in 1979/80 in limited over matches only. McKenzie toured England in 1961, 1964 and 1968. He played 13 of his 60 Tests for Australia in England, bagging 53 wickets (av. 29.66), scoring 121 runs (av. 8.64) and holding 3 catches. His best bowling and batting performances were 7 for 153 at Old Trafford in 1964 and 34 at Lord's in 1961. His best tour of England was in 1968, when he bagged 88 wickets (av. 22.45) and took 29 Test wickets (av. 22.55). McKenzie was the youngest Test bowler to achieve the 100, 150 and 200 wicket milestones in his playing career. *Above right:* Born in Sydney in 1936, the right-handed top order batsman, leg-break and googly bowler and fine slip fielder Bobby Simpson toured England in 1961 and 1964. He represented New South Wales from 1952/53 to 1977/78 in 67 matches and Western Australia from 1956/57 to 1960/61 in 24 matches. Simpson played 10 of his 62 Tests in England, accumulating 649 runs (av. 46.36), bagging 8 wickets (av. 48.50) and holding 17 catches. His best batting performance in England was a mammoth 311 at Old Trafford in 1964. The highest individual innings in a Test match on the ground against England during the same innings, he added 201 for the first wicket with Bill Lawry. His best bowling figures of 4 for 23 in fact came in the same match. Simpson's best tour of England was in 1961, when he amassed 1,947 runs (av. 51.23). In his following tour as captain of the side he scored 1,714 runs (av. 57.13). His career-best score was 359 for New South Wales versus Queensland at Brisbane in 1963/64. After retiring from the game in 1989 he returned to England as coach of the Australian tourists and in 1991 he was appointed cricket manager of Leicestershire. Since 2000 he has coached Lancashire.

Born in Mackay, Queensland in 1927, a lower order right-handed batsman and wicketkeeper, Wally Grout toured England in 1961 and 1964. He represented Australia in 10 of his 51 Tests in England, scoring 131 runs (av. 11.91) and taking 31 dismissals (30 catches and 1 stumping). His highest score was 37 at Headingley in 1964. Grout played 94 matches for Queensland from 1946/47 to 1965/66 and he was regarded as one of the greatest of all Australian wicketkeepers. In 1961 he achieved a then record 23 dismissals in Tests against England. He suffered from heart failure in 1964 and died four years later in the Wickham district of Brisbane.

Richie Benaud (*left*) and Bobby Simpson (*right*) walk towards the wicket at Scarborough during the cricket festival match against Mr T.N. Pearce's XI in 1961.

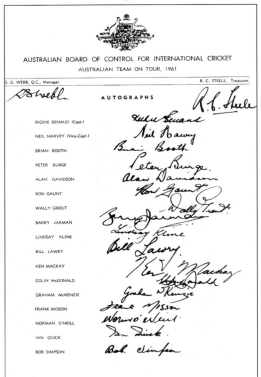

AUSTRALIAN BOARD OF CONTROL FOR INTERNATIONAL CRICKET

AUSTRALIAN TEAM ON TOUR, 1961

S. G. WEBB, Q.C., Manager.   R. C. STEELE, Treasurer.

AUTOGRAPHS

RICHIE BENAUD (Capt.)

NEIL HARVEY (Vice-Capt.)

BRIAN BOOTH

PETER BURGE

ALAN DAVIDSON

RON GAUNT

WALLY GROUT

BARRY JARMAN

LINDSAY KLINE

BILL LAWRY

KEN MACKAY

COLIN McDONALD

GRAHAM McKENZIE

FRANK MISSON

NORMAN O'NEILL

IAN QUICK

BOB SIMPSON

Scarborough Cricket Festival

President : H.R.H. THE DUKE OF EDINBURGH, K.G.

T. N. PEARCE'S XI v. AUSTRALIA

Played on the Scarborough Cricket Ground on September 6th, 7th and 8th, 1961

T. N. PEARCE'S XI

			First Innings		Second Innings	
1	J. H. Edrich	(Surrey)	st Jarman b Kline	110	c Benaud b Simpson	20
2	G. J. Smith	(Essex)	c Jarman b McKenzie	8	st Jarman b Mackay	100
3	M. J. K. Smith	(Warwick)	c McKenzie b Quick	2	c Booth b Mackay	30
4	E. R. Dexter	(Sussex)	c Simpson b Mackay	57	b Mackay	110
5	P. B. H. May (Capt)	(Surrey)	b Mackay	100	c & b Kline	41
6	J. M. Parks (WK)	(Sussex)	c & b Benaud	2	c O'Neill b Benaud	60
7	T. E. Bailey	(Essex)	c O'Neill b Benaud	4	not out	7
8	D. A. Allen	(Glos)	b Mackay	3		
9	F. S. Trueman	(Yorks)	not out	60		
10	M. H. J. Allen	(Northants)	not out	8		
11	J. D. F. Larter	(Northants)				
			b 1 lb 7 w...	8	b 4 lb 1 w... nb...	5

Total (8 wkts. dec.) 375   Total (6 wkts. dec.) 373

Fall of the Wickets

1	2	3	4	5	6	7	8	9	10	1	2	3	4	5	6	7	8	9	10
13	99	105	202	209	235	262	359	...	40	188	235	295	347	373					

Analysis of Bowling

	First Innings			Second Innings		
	Overs	Mdns.	Runs	Wkts.	Overs	Mdns.	Runs	Wkts.
Gaunt	6		23		8	2	12	
McKenzie	5	3	7	1	9	2	35	
Mackay	24	1	136	3	29	4	110	4
Quick	8		44	1				
Kline	13	3	60	1	11	1	48	1
Benaud	13	1	59	2				
Simpson	4		38		15		139	1
O'Neill					7	1	24	

AUSTRALIA

			First Innings		Second Innings	
1	R. Benaud (Capt)		c Parks b Trueman	1	c Parks b Dexter	41
2	R. B. Simpson		b Trueman	28	b Allen M	121
3	N. C. O'Neill		c Dexter b Allen D A	63	b Dexter	34
4	P. J. Burge		c Allen D b Allen M...	71	b Trueman	49
5	B. C. Booth		c Allen D b Trueman	77	b Trueman	38
6	K. Mackay		c Edrich b Allen D	33	c Allen D b Allen M...	14
7	G. D. McKenzie		b Trueman	1	not out	16
8	B. N. Jarman (w.k.)		c Bailey	80	c Edrich b Allen D	21
9	L. W. Quick		b Bailey	17	not out	1
10	L. F. Kline		c Allen M b Bailey	16		
11	R. A. Gaunt		b Allen M	2	b... lb 8 w 1 nb...	9
			b 3 lb... w... nb...	3		

Total..... 392   Total..... 359

Fall of the Wickets

1	2	3	4	5	6	7	8	9	10	1	2	3	4	5	6	7	8	9	10
3	68	143	165	238	312	314	360	378	392	100	177	213	283	292	318	348			

Analysis of Bowling

	First Innings			Second Innings		
	Overs	Mdns.	Runs	Wkts.	Overs	Mdns.	Runs	Wkts.
Trueman	13		59	4	16	1	75	2
Larter	8		35		7		40	
Bailey	12	2	50	2	4		32	
Dexter	6	1	25		15	1	70	2
Allen M H J	17	3	102	2	16	2	80	2
Allen D A	15	2	118	2	12.1		53	1

Umpires : J. S. Buller, D. Davies.   Scorers : H. L. Walker, J. Cameron

Wickets Pitched 11 a.m.   Lunch 1-30 p.m.   Tea 4-15 p.m.   Stumps Drawn 5-30 p.m.

A New Ball may be taken at the option of the fielding Captain, after 85 overs or 200 runs

Wright & Co. Ltd., 15 North Street, Scarborough.

Left: The Australians tour autograph sheet of 1961. *Right:* A copy of the completed scorecard of Mr T.N. Pearce's XI versus the touring Australians at Scarborough Cricket Festival, North Marine Road, Scarborough on 6, 7 and 8 September 1961. The Australians won by 3 wickets.

The Australian touring party of 1964. From left to right, back row: A.E. James (masseur), R.M. Cowper, J. Potter, I.R. Redpath, R.H.D. Sellers, T. Veivers, D. Sherwood (scorer). Middle row: N.J.N. Hawke, G.D. McKenzie, W.M. Lawry, J.A. Ledward (treasurer), A.N. Connolly, G.E. Corling, J.W. Martin. Front row: B.N. Jarman, P.J.P. Burge, R.B. Simpson (captain), R.C. Steele (manager), B.C. Booth (vice-captain), N.C. O'Neill, A.T.W. Grout. The 1964 Australian side played 30 first-class matches, winning 11, losing 3 and drawing 16. They also played 6 second-class matches with 3 wins, 1 loss and 2 draws. The Test match series saw a 5-Test rubber with 1 win, 0 losses and 4 drawn Tests.

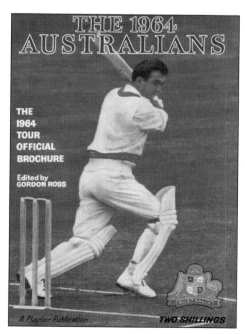

The cover of the official tour brochure for 1964, published by Playfair Publications, depicting Bobby Simpson in action.

Born in Geelong, Victoria in 1941, Ian Redpath *(left)* was a sound right-handed opening batsman, right-arm medium pace bowler and good short leg fielder. He played 92 matches for Victoria from 1961/62 to 1975/76 and he toured England in 1964 and 1968. He played 10 of his 66 Tests in England, scoring 526 runs (av. 30.94), with a top score of 92 at Headingley in 1968, and he held 12 catches. His best tour of England was in 1968, when he hit 1,474 runs (av. 43.35. His career-best score was 261 for Victoria against Queensland at Melbourne Cricket Ground in 1962/63. He was awarded an MBE for his services to cricket after retiring from the game. Born in the Cheltenham district of Adelaide in 1939, Neil Hawke *(right)* was a right-handed lower order batsman and right-arm medium-fast bowler who represented three Australian State teams between 1959/60 and 1968/69. He played 7 matches for Western Australia in 1959/60, 60 matches for South Australia from 1960/61 to 1967/68 and 2 matches for Tasmania in 1968/69. Hawke toured England in 1964 and 1968 and played 7 of his 27 Tests in England. He scored 73 runs (av. 14.60), bagged 19 wickets (av. 32.16) and he held 3 catches. His best batting and bowling performances were 37 at Headingley in 1964 and 6 for 47 at Kennington Oval in 1964. His most successful tour to England was in 1964, when he bagged 83 wickets (av. 19.80) including 18 in 5 Tests. He died on Christmas Day 2000.

Born in Skipton, Victoria in 1939, Alan Connolly was a right-arm fast-medium bowler and late order right-handed batsman. He represented Victoria 83 times from 1959/60 to 1970/71 and Middlesex 44 times between 1969 and 1970 and he toured England in 1964 and 1968. He played 5 of his 29 Tests in England, bagging 23 wickets (av. 25.70), scoring 5 runs (av. 1.67) and holding a single catch. His best performances were 5 for 72 at Headingley in 1968 and 3 at Kennington Oval in 1968. In 1969 he bagged 74 wickets (av. 23.24) for Middlesex and his best career bowling performance was 9 for 67 for Victoria against Queensland at Brisbane in 1964/65.

Born in the Carlton district of Sydney in 1937, Norman O'Neill was a right-handed attacking middle order batsman, right-arm medium or leg-break bowler and excellent deep fielder. O'Neill represented New South Wales 70 times between 1955/56 and 1966/67 and toured England in 1961 and 1964. He played in 9 of his 42 Tests in England scoring 480 runs (av. 36.92) with a best performance of 117 at Kennington Oval in 1961. His best bowling was 0 for 13 at Kennington Oval in 1961 and he held 7 catches. His best tour of England was in 1961, when he accumulated 1,981 runs (av. 60.03). His career-best score was 284 for the touring Australians against the President's XI at Ahmedabad, India in 1959/60. His final first-class game was for the Prime Minister's XI in the Koyna Relief Fund match in India in 1967/68.

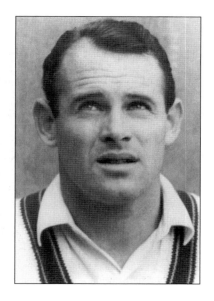

The Australian touring party 1968 signatures on a miniature cricket bat. The 1968 Australian side played 26 first-class matches, winning 8, losing 3 and drawing 14, with 1 match abandoned. They also played 4 second-class matches with 2 wins and 2 drawn matches. The Test match series saw a 5-Test rubber with 1 win, 1 loss and 3 drawn Tests.

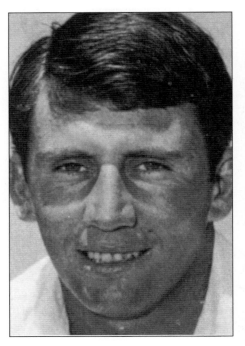

Born in the Unley district of Adelaide in 1943, Ian 'Chappelli' Chappell was an excellent right-handed middle order batsman, leg-break and googly bowler and excellent slip fielder. He represented South Australia 109 times from 1961/62 to 1979/80 and Lancashire in a single match in 1963. He played 14 of his 75 Tests in England during his tours in 1968, 1972 and 1975. He accumulated 1,111 runs (av. 46.29), with a top score of 192 at Kennington Oval in 1975, bagged 3 wickets (av. 64.33) with a best of 1 for 26 at Headingley in 1975 and he held 9 catches. He achieved 1,000 runs on each of his tours of England, with a best of 1,261 runs (av. 48.50) in 1968. He was captain of the 1972 and 1975 touring parties and captained Australia in 30 of his 75 Tests. His highest score was his 209 for the touring Australians against Barbados in Bridgetown in 1972/73 and, after coming out of retirement to play for Kerry Packer's World Series Cricket in 1977, he later became a well-known and respected television commentator for Channel 9. He was the grandson of V.Y. 'Vic' Richardson and elder brother of G.S. 'Greg' and T.M. 'Trevor' Chappell who all played for Australia.

Born in Dungog, New South Wales in 1945, Doug Walters was an attacking right-handed middle order batsman and right-arm medium pace bowler who represented New South Wales in 103 matches from 1962/63 to 1980/81. Walters toured England in 1968, 1972, 1975 and 1977 and he played 18 of his 74 Tests in England, scoring 745 runs (av. 25.89) with a highest innings of 88 at Old Trafford in 1977. He also took 5 wickets (av. 16.80), with a best performance of 4 for 34 at Kennington Oval in 1975, and he held 14 catches. His best tour of England came in 1975, when he scored 784 runs (av. 60.30). His career-best score was 253 for New South Wales versus South Australia at the Adelaide Oval in 1964/65. Having retired from the game, he has been awarded an MBE and he has acted as a supporters' tour guide to England during previous recent tours by Australia to England.

AUSTRALIAN BOARD OF CONTROL FOR INTERNATIONAL CRICKET
AUSTRALIAN TEAM ON TOUR, 1968

R. J. PARISH, Manager.   L. E. TRUMAN, Treasurer.

AUTOGRAPHS

BILL LAWRY (Capt.)

BARRY JARMAN (Vice-Capt.)

IAN CHAPPELL

ALAN CONNOLLY

BOB COWPER

ERIC FREEMAN

JOHN GLEESON

NEIL HAWKE

JOHN INVERARITY

LES. JOSLIN

ASHLEY MALLETT

GRAHAM McKENZIE

DAVE RENNEBERG

IAN REDPATH

PAUL SHEAHAN

BRIAN TABER

DOUG. WALTERS

D. SHERWOOD (Scorer).   A. E. JAMES (Physiotherapist).

The 1968 autographed team sheet.

Born in the Chatswood district of Sydney in 1945, Ashley Mallett, like Doug Walters, toured England in 1968, 1972, 1975 and 1980. He played 91 matches for South Australia from 1967/68 to 1980/81 as an off-break bowler and late order right-handed batsman. He played in 8 of his 38 Tests in England taking 26 wickets (av. 34.81), scoring 100 runs (av. 20.00) and holding 5 catches. His best performance with the bat was 43 not out at Kennington Oval in 1968 and with the ball was 5 for 114 at Headingley in 1972. Since retiring he has coached and written books on the game of cricket.

Six

Massie, Lillee and Thomson 1972 to 1981

Dennis Lillee was born in Subiaco, Perth in 1949. A right-arm fast bowler and right-handed late order batsman, he represented Western Australia 76 times between 1969/70 and 1983/84, Tasmania 6 times in 1987/88 and Northamptonshire 7 times in 1988. An awesome fast bowler, he toured England in 1972, 1975, 1980 and 1981. He played 16 of his 70 Tests in England, scoring 278 runs with a top score of 73 not out at Lord's in 1975 and bagging 96 wickets (av. 20.56), with a best haul of 7 for 89 at Kennington Oval in 1981. He also held a single catch. Without any doubt the best fast bowler of his generation to have graced the Test arena, his tally of 355 Test wickets was surpassed by Ian Botham in August 1986. His best tour of England was in 1972, when he achieved 53 wickets (av. 22.58), including 31 Test wickets (av. 17.67) in the 6 Test series. He returned to England to act as bowling coach for Northamptonshire and has also been involved in fast bowling seminars and coaching all around the cricket world. He was awarded an MBE for his services to the game of cricket.

Born in Unley, Adelaide in 1948, Greg Chappell was a stylish right-handed middle order batsman, right-arm medium pace bowler and excellent slip fielder. He represented South Australia 57 times between 1966/67 and 1972/73, Somerset 52 times from 1968 to 1969 and Queensland in 61 matches between 1973/74 and 1983/84. He toured England in 1972, 1975, 1977 and 1980 and played 15 of his 87 Tests in England, scoring 1,020 runs (av. 40.80), bagging 2 wickets (av. 142.50) and holding 23 catches. His best performances were 131 at Lord's in 1972 and 1 for 28 at Old Trafford in 1972. His best tour of England was his first, in 1972, when he amassed 1,260 runs (av. 70.00), including 437 runs in Tests (av. 48.55). His career-best score was 247 not out for Australia versus New Zealand at the Basin Reserve, Wellington in 1973/74 and he, like his elder brother Ian, played World Series Cricket in Australia from 1977 to 1979. He captained Australia in 48 of his 87 Tests and since retiring has been awarded an MBE for his services to the game, and has become a respected cricket writer and commentator.

Rodney Marsh was born in the Armadale district of Perth in 1947. A left-handed middle order attacking batsman, occasional off-break bowler and wicketkeeper, he played 97 matches for his native Western Australia from 1968/69 to 1983/84. Marsh was without doubt Australia's greatest wicketkeepers and he toured England in 1972, 1975, 1977, 1980 and 1981. He played 21 of his 96 Tests in England, achieving 71 dismissals (68 catches and 3 stumpings) and scoring 773 runs (av. 24.94), with a top score of 91 at Old Trafford in 1972. He achieved 104 on his first-class debut for Western Australia against the touring West Indians at the WACA Ground, Perth in 1968/69 and four seasons later made his career-best score of 236 for Western Australia on the same ground against the touring Pakistanis in 1972/73. Since retiring he was awarded an MBE for his services to the game of cricket and he has served as the head coach of the Australian Cricket Academy in Adelaide, where many new cricket names and talented young players have been assisted by his cricket skills. His son Daniel has represented Tasmania and in 2001 he is Leicestershire's overseas cricketer.

A regular occurrence during Australian tours to England is the customary team dinner, staged by The National Sporting Club at The Café Royal in London W1. Seen here is the menu cover for the Australian cricket touring team dinner of 1972, staged on 27 June.

The Australian touring party of 1977.

Born in Inverell, New South Wales in 1946, Rick McCosker was a sound right-handed opening batsman who represented New South Wales in 86 matches between 1973/74 and 1983/84. He played 9 of his 25 Tests for Australia in England, scoring 669 runs (av. 47.79), with a top score of 127 at Kennington Oval in 1975 and also held 6 catches. His best tour of England was in 1975, when he scored 1,078 runs (av. 59.88).

Born in Waratah, New South Wales in 1951, Gary Gilmour was a left-handed middle order batsman, left-arm medium pace bowler and useful close fielder. He represented New South Wales in 42 matches from 1971/72 and 1979/80 and he toured England once in 1975, playing in just the one Test at Headingley. In that Test he scored 6 runs (av. 6.00), with a top score of 6, bagged 9 wickets (av. 17.44), with a best of 6 for 85, and he held 6 catches. He scored 122 on his first-class debut for New South Wales against South Australia at Sydney in 1971/72.

Born in Greenacre, Sydney in 1950, Jeff Thomson was a very quick right-arm fast bowler and right-handed lower order batsman. He represented New South Wales 7 times from 1972/73 to 1973/74, Queensland 86 times between 1974/75 and 1985/86 and Middlesex in 8 matches in 1981. Thomson played 11 of his 51 Tests in England, achieving 42 wickets (av. 31.31), with a best haul of 5 for 38 at Edgbaston in 1975. He scored 179 runs (av. 16.27), with a top score of 49 at Edgbaston in 1975 and he held 4 catches. With Lillee, Thomson formed one of the best opening bowling attacks that Test Cricket has witnessed during the 1970s and 1980s. Since retiring from the game, he has coached various sides, most recently the Zimbabweans in the West Indies and England in 2000, and he has acted as a television and radio commentator on the game around the world.

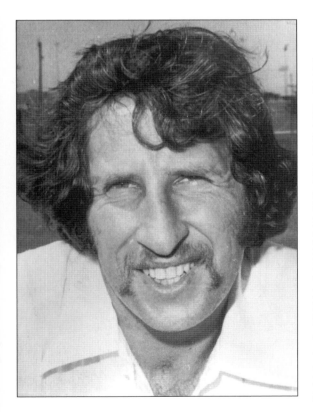

Born in West Hobart, Tasmania in 1948 Max Walker, nicknamed 'Tangles', was a right-arm medium pace bowler and lower order right-handed hard hitting batsman who represented Victoria in 70 matches from 1968/69 to 1981/82. Walker played 9 of his 34 Tests in England. He scored 176 runs (av. 16.00) with a top score of 78 not out at Kennington Oval in 1977, bagged 28 wickets (av. 37.04), with a best performance of 5 for 48 at Edgbaston in 1975, and he held 2 catches. His best tour of England was in 1977, when he achieved 53 wickets (av. 22.33). Since retiring from the game, he has written several humorous books on the game and has worked on both television and radio in Australia. He was one of the last Australian cricketers to have also played Australian Rules Football professionally for Hawthorn.

Born in the Cottesloe district of Perth in 1942, Ross Edwards was a middle order right-handed batsman and occasional wicketkeeper who represented Western Australia 71 times between 1964/65 and 1974/75 and New South Wales in 5 matches in 1979/80. Edwards played 8 of his 20 Tests in England and he toured in 1972 and 1975. He scored 544 runs (av. 49.95), with a top score of 170 not out at Trent Bridge in 1972. His best bowling performance was 0 for 20 at Kennington Oval in 1975 and he held a single catch.

The Australian touring party signatures in 1977 on a Stuart Surridge miniature cricket bat.

Born in Hurstville, Sydney in 1949, Kerry O'Keeffe was a leg-break and googly bowler and right-handed late order batsman who played 65 matches for New South Wales between 1968/69 and 1979/80 and 46 matches for Somerset from 1971 to 1972. He played 3 of his 24 Tests in England, scoring 125 runs (av. 62.50) with a highest score of 48 not out at Trent Bridge in 1977. He also took 3 wickets (av. 101.67), with a best of 1 for 25 at Old Trafford in 1977, and he held 3 catches. He only toured once, in 1977, when he bagged 36 wickets (av. 28.75), a tally which was some way below his haul in 1972 whilst playing domestic county cricket for Somerset when he achieved 77 wickets (av. 23.57).

Born in Nedlands, Perth in 1951, Craig Serjeant was a right-handed middle order batsman who represented his native Western Australia in 51 matches from 1976/77 to 1982/83. Serjeant played 3 of his 12 Tests in England scoring 106 runs (av. 21.20) with a top score of 81 at Lord's in 1977 and he held a single catch. He toured England just the once, in 1977, when he scored 663 runs (av. 33.15), with a highest score of 159 versus Nottinghamshire at Trent Bridge.

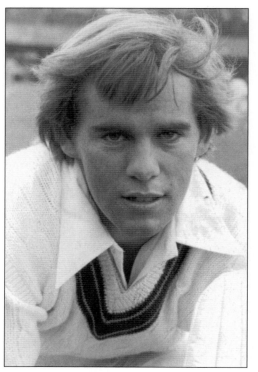

Born in the Mile End district of Adelaide in 1955. David Hookes was a left-handed middle order attacking batsman and left-arm slow to medium bowler who represented South Australia 130 times between 1975/76 and 1991/92. Hookes played 5 of his 23 Tests in England scoring 283 runs (av. 31.44) with a top score of 85 at Kennington Oval in 1977 and he held a single catch. He toured England just once, in 1977, when he scored 804 runs (av. 32.16), with a highest score of 108 against Somerset at Bath. His 107 scored off 34 balls for South Australia versus Victoria at Adelaide in 1982/83 was at the time the fastest century scored in first-class cricket in terms of balls received. His career-best score of 306 not out for South Australia against Tasmania at Adelaide in 1986/87 came after he had added 462 unfinished for the fourth wicket with Wayne Phillips, which was then the highest partnership by any pair of Australian batsman. Since retiring from the game Hookes has concentrated on cricket writing and television and radio commentary.

Born in Margaret River, Western Australia in 1954, Kim Hughes was a right-handed middle order batsman and right-arm medium pace bowler. He represented Western Australia on 66 occasions between 1975/76 and 1988/89 and Natal in South African domestic matches between 1989/90 and 1990/91. Hughes played 8 of his 70 Tests in England, scoring 502 runs (av. 33.47) with a top score of 117 at Lord's in the Centenary Test in 1980, and he also held 3 catches. He led Australia in 28 of his 70 Tests and scored 119 on his first-class debut for Western Australia versus New South Wales at the WACA, Perth in 1975/76.

Ray Bright was born in the Footscray district of Melbourne in 1954. A right-handed lower order batsman and slow left-arm bowler, he represented Victoria 114 times from 1972/73 to 1987/88. Bright played 9 of his 25 Tests in England, bagging 17 wickets (av. 37.12), with a best bowling performance of 5 for 68 at Edgbaston in 1981. He scored 169 runs (av. 13.00), with a top score of 33 at Lord's in 1981, and he held 7 catches. His best tour of England was his first, in 1977, when he finished the season with 39 wickets (av. 20.35). He did not improve upon this performance during either of his next two tours in 1980 and 1981.

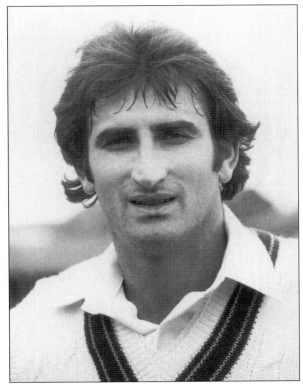

Len Pascoe was born in Bridgetown North, Western Australian in 1950. A right-arm quickie, he played 4 of his 14 Tests in England, achieving 19 wickets (av. 26.05), with a best haul of 5 for 59 at Lord's in 1980. A late order right-handed batsman, he scored 23 runs (av. 7.67), with a top score of 20 at Trent Bridge in 1977. Pascoe played 54 matches for New South Wales between 1974/75 and 1983/84 and he toured England in 1977 and 1980. He took 41 wickets (av. 21.78) in 1977 and 17 wickets (av. 26.17) in 1980.

The Australian touring party of 1980.

Allan Border played 25 of his 130 Tests for Australia in England, starting with the Centenary Test at Lord's, London in 1980. He amassed 2,082 runs (av. 65.06) with a highest score of 200 not out at Headingley in 1993, and he held 37 catches. Less significant was his bowling, returning 1 wicket (av. 116.00) with a best of 1 for 16 at Lord's, London in 1993. In addition to his highest score of 200 not out, he scored 4 other Test hundreds in England, 123 not out at Old Trafford and 106 not out at Kennington Oval both in 1981, 196 at Lord's and 146 not out at Old Trafford both in 1985. Border represented New South Wales 25 times between 1976/77 and 1979/80, Gloucestershire once in 1977, Queensland 68 times between 1980/81 and 1991/92 and Essex 40 times between 1986 and 1988. Since retirement he has been involved in television commentary and has had a ground named after him in Brisbane, 'The Allan Border Oval', which has been used by Queensland for domestic first-class and limited over matches.

Born in East Freemantle, Perth in 1956, left-handed opening batsman Graeme Wood played in 12 of his 59 Tests in England, scoring 112 in his first Test in England, at Lord's in the Centenary Test in 1980. In total he scored 690 runs (av. 31.36), with a top score of 172 at Trent Bridge in 1985 and he held 6 catches. He represented Western Australia 125 times as a left-handed opening batsman and right-arm medium pace bowler between 1976/77 and 1991/92 and he toured England three times in 1980, 1981 and 1985. His best tour was in 1981, when he scored 690 runs (av. 31.36).

Graham Yallop was born in Balwyn, Melbourne in 1952. A left-handed top order batsman, he toured England twice in 1980 and 1981 and played 7 of his 39 Tests in England, scoring 318 runs (av. 24.46), with a top score of 114 at Old Trafford in 1981 and he also held 7 catches. His best bowling performance, 0 for 17, was achieved at Kennington Oval in 1981. His career-best score was 268 for Australia versus Pakistan at Melbourne in 1983/84 and he played a total of 87 matches for Victoria between 1972/73 and 1984/85.

John Dyson was born in Kogarah, Sydney in 1954. A right-handed opening batsman, he played 5 of his 30 Tests in England, scoring 206 runs (av. 20.60) with a highest score of 102 at Headingley in 1971 and he also held 2 catches. He represented New South Wales 94 times between 1975/76 and 1988/89 and he toured England in 1980 and 1981. His most successful tour of England came in 1981, when he amassed 582 runs (av. 30.63) and his career-best score was 241 for New South Wales versus South Australia at Adelaide in 1983/84.

Born in Summer Hill, Sydney in 1959, Dirk Wellham is seen here in action against Middlesex at Lord's as Clive Radley and Keith Brown look on. He was a right-handed middle order batsman who played 2 of his 6 Tests in England. He scored 145 runs (av. 36.25), with a top score of 103 at Kennington Oval in 1981, and he held a single catch. He played 68 matches for New South Wales between 1980/81 and 1987/88, 32 for Tasmania between 1988/89 and 1990/91 and 10 for Queensland in 1991/92. His best tour of England was his second visit in 1985, when he scored 669 runs (av. 55.75).

AUSTRALIAN CRICKET BOARD
CENTENARY TEST TOUR OF ENGLAND 1980

Manager: P. L. RIDINGS
Hon. Medical: Dr. D. CARNEY
Physiotherapist: M. MASON
Scorer: D. K. SHERWOOD

WALDORF HOTEL
ALDWYCH,
LONDON

AUTOGRAPHS

G. CHAPPELL (Captain)

K. HUGHES (Vice-Captain)

A. BORDER

R. BRIGHT

G. DYMOCK

J. DYSON

B. LAIRD

D. LILLEE

A. MALLETT

R. MARSH

L. PASCOE

J. THOMSON

G. WOOD

G. YALLOP

AUSTRALIAN CRICKET BOARD

Autograph sheet for the 1980 Australian Cricket Board Centenary Test tour of England.

Born in Wagga Wagga, New South Wales in 1957, right-arm fast-medium pace bowler and right-handed late order batsman Geoffrey Lawson played 15 of his 46 Tests in England for Australia. He bagged 63 wickets (av. 30.25), with a best haul of 7 for 81 at Lord's in 1981 and he scored 272 runs (av. 17.00) with a top score of 74 at Lord's in 1989. He played 115 times for New South Wales between 1977/78 and 1991/92 and a single match for Lancashire in 1979 and he toured England three times in 1981, 1985 and 1989. During the 1985 tour he took 22 Test wickets (av. 37.72) and in 1989 he took 29 Test wickets (av. 27.27).

110

Born in Subiaco, Perth in 1956, Terry Alderman played 12 of his 41 Tests in England. He had great success as a right-arm fast medium pace opening bowler, bagging 83 wickets (av. 19.34) in 1989. The Western Australia bowler's best performance was 6 for 128 at Lord's in 1989 during a series when he always seemed to dismiss England batsman Graham Gooch. Alderman was a right-handed tail end batsman and he scored 42 runs (av. 8.40) with a top score of 12 not out at Trent Bridge in 1981 and he held 10 catches. Alderman represented Western Australia 103 times between 1974/75 and 1991/92, Kent 40 times between 1984 and 1986 and Gloucestershire 20 times in 1988. He toured England in 1981 and 1989 but his best season in England was for Kent in 1986, when he bagged 98 wickets (av. 19.20).

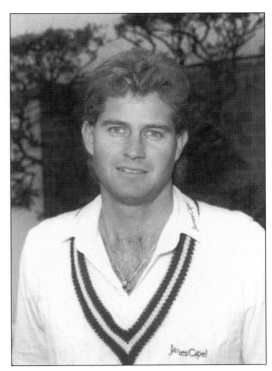

Born in Richmond, Melbourne in 1951, right-arm quick bowler Rodney Hogg played 2 of his 38 Tests in England in 1981 on his only tour. He took 4 wickets (av. 30.75), with a best of 3 for 47 at Trent Bridge in 1981, and he made his highest score of 0 not out with the bat at Edgbaston in 1981. During his domestic career in Australia, Hogg represented South Australia 39 times between 1975/76 and 1983/84 and Victoria twice in 1984/85. During the tour of England in 1981, he took 27 wickets (av. 24.33) some way below his performance of 41 wickets (av. 12.85), when England had visited Australia in 1978/79.

Allan Border chuckles to himself as a male streaker is led away by the local constabulary at Edgbaston in 1981. Rodney Marsh, the Australian wicketkeeper, had caught the pitch invader.

Born in Surry Hills, Sydney in 1959, left-arm pace bowler Mike Whitney was drafted into the Australian side in 1981 while he was acting as overseas player for Gloucestershire due to injuries in the touring party. He played 2 of his 9 Tests during that summer, taking 5 wickets (av. 49.20) with a best of 2 for 50 at Old Trafford and he scored 4 runs (av. 1.00) with a top score of 4 at Kennington Oval. Since retiring he has acted as a television commentator on the game and is a keen collector of cricket memorabilia.

Seven

Border Years 1985 to 1989

The Australian touring party of 1989. From left to right, back row: M.K. Walsh (scorer), M.R.J. Veletta, M.A. Taylor, M.G. Hughes, T.M. Alderman, T.M. Moody, C.G. Rackemann, G.F. Lawson, T.B.A. May, G.D. Campbell, T.V. Hohns, R.B. Simpson (coach). Front row: T.J. Zoehrer, D.C. Boon, G.R. Marsh (vice-captain), L.M. Sawle (manager), A.R. Border (captain), D.M. Jones, S.R. Waugh, I.A. Healy.

Born in Launceston, Tasmania in 1960, David Boon, a middle order right-handed batsman, played 16 of his 63 Tests in England, scoring 1,121 runs (av. 48.74) and he held 18 catches usually at slip or short-leg. His best batting performance came at cricket's headquarters, Lord's, in 1993, when he amassed 164 not out. Boon later captained Durham in English county cricket, but with little success. Since retiring he has served Tasmania as coach and was awarded an MBE for his services to sport.

The Australian touring party autograph sheet of 1985.

Born in Deniliquin, New South Wales in 1963, Victorian right-handed all-rounder and part-time Australian Rules Footballer Simon O'Donnell played 5 of his 6 Tests in England. He scored 184 runs (av. 26.29), with a top score of 48, at Lord's in 1985, bagged 6 wickets (av. 81.17) with a best haul of 3 for 37 at Headingley in 1985 and he held 3 catches. O'Donnell played for Victoria 61 times between 1983/84 and 1991/92, and even played a season of minor county cricket for Northumberland in 1989 when he was not fortunate enough to have been selected on the Australian tour of England that particular summer. He missed the 1987/88 domestic season in Australian due to cancer, but was fully recovered by the following season.

Born in Newcastle, New South Wales in 1959, Greg Matthews was a left-handed middle order batsman and off-break bowler. He played just 1 of his 28 Tests in England, at Old Trafford in 1985, scoring 21 runs (av. 10.50) with a top score of 17 and with a best bowling score of 0 for 21. He represented New South Wales 90 times between 1982/83 and 1991/92.

AUSTRALIAN CRICKET TOUR 1989
Official sponsors CASTLEMAINE XXXX

Manager - L. Sawle   Coach - R. B. Simpson   Captain - A. R. Border   Vice-Captain - G. R. Marsh

OFFICIAL AUTOGRAPH SHEET

A. R. BORDER
(Captain)

G. R. MARSH
(Vice-Captain)

T.M. ALDERMAN

D. C. BOON

G. D. CAMPBELL

I. HEALY

T. V. HOHNS

M. G. HUGHES

D. M. JONES

G. F. LAWSON

T. B. MAY

T. M. MOODY

C. G. RACKEMANN

M. A. TAYLOR

M. R. VELETTA

S. R. WAUGH

T. J. ZOEHRER

L. SAWLE
(Manager)

R. B. SIMPSON
(Coach)

XXXX AUSSIE CRICKETCALL 0898-12-14-40 for all the latest tour news
(calls charged at 38p per minute – peak, and 25p per minute – off-peak, including VAT)

The Australian touring party autograph sheet of 1989.

Born in Ipswich, Queensland in 1965, Craig McDermott, a right-arm quickie, played 8 of his 36 Tests in England. He bagged 30 wickets (av. 34.23) with a best performance of 8 for 141 at Old Trafford in 1981. As a right-handed late order batsman, he scored 111 runs (av. 12.33), with a highest innings of 35 at Edgbaston in 1985 and he held 2 catches. On the 1985 tour of England he bagged 30 Test wickets (av. 30.03), and on the tour he achieved 51 wickets (av. 31.54). McDermott signed as Yorkshire's overseas player in 1992, but had to decline at a later date due to injury.

Born in Stanthorpe, Queensland in 1960, Greg Ritchie played 6 of his 30 Tests in England as a right-handed middle order batsman, touring only once. He scored 422 runs (av. 42.20), with a top score of 146 at Trent Bridge in 1985 and he held 3 catches. His best bowling was 0 for 10 at Trent Bridge in 1985. He played minor county cricket for Buckinghamshire in 1979 and having retired from the game he has acted as a television comic on cricket known as 'MaHatMaCoat' on Channel 9's cricket programme.

A right-handed opening batsman hailing from Western Australia, Geoff Marsh was born in Northam in 1958. He represented Western Australia 90 times from 1977/78 to 1991/92 and played 6 of his 50 Tests in England. He amassed 347 runs (av. 31.55), with a top score of 138 at Trent Bridge in 1989, and he held 5 catches. He and Mark Taylor created a record new first wicket partnership for Australia against England at Trent Bridge in 1989 when they added 329. Marsh's career-best score was 355 not out for Western Australia versus South Australia at the WACA Ground, Perth in 1989/90. Since retiring he has worked as coach for both Australia and Western Australia.

Born in the Spring Hill district of Brisbane in 1964, Queensland wicketkeeper and right-handed middle order batsman Ian 'Heals' Healy played 18 of his 64 Tests in England, scoring 624 runs (av. 31.20) with a top score of 102 not out at Old Trafford in 1993. He achieved 67 dismissals (60 catches and 7 stumpings). He toured England in 1989, 1993 and 1997 and he represented his native Queensland in domestic Australian cricket. Since returning he has worked as a television commentator on the game.

Born in Euroa, Victoria in 1961, Merv Hughes, the right-arm Victorian fast bowler and right-handed late order batsman with the big moustache, played 12 of his 37 Tests in England. He bagged 50 wickets (av. 29.20), with a best performance of 5 for 92 at Trent Bridge in 1993, and he scored 203 runs (av. 20.30) with a top score of 71 at Headingley in 1989. Hughes represented his native Victoria from 1981/82 and he even played one match for Essex in 1983.

Born in Coburg, Melbourne in 1961, Victorian right-handed top order batsman Dean 'Deano' Jones played 6 of his 49 Tests in England. He amassed 566 runs (av. 70.75) and held 4 catches. His best score was 157 at Edgbaston in 1989. Jones played as overseas player for Durham during their inaugural season in 1992 with Ian Botham, Wayne Larkins, David Graveney and Simon Hughes. His best tour of England was in 1989 when he topped the tour batting averages with 1,510 runs (av. 88.82). His highest score in England was his 248 for the touring Australians against Warwickshire at Edgbaston in 1989.

South Australian right-arm spinner and right-handed tail end batsman Tim May was born in North Adelaide in 1962 and he represented South Australia from 1984/85 in domestic Australian cricket. He played 5 of his 7 Tests in England, bagging 21 wickets (av. 28.19) with a best haul of 5 for 89 at Edgbaston in 1993, and he scored 23 runs (av. 11.50), with a top score of 15 at Kennington Oval in 1993. He also held 2 catches.

Mark 'Tails' Taylor was born in Leeton, New South Wales in 1964. A sound left-handed opening batsman, he played 18 of his 60 Tests in England. He accumulated 1,584 runs (av. 52.80) and held 22 catches, mainly at slip. His best performance was achieved at Trent Bridge in 1989, when he scored 219 and shared an opening wicket record stand of 329 with fellow opening batsman Geoff Marsh, who scored 138. In addition to his highest score at Trent Bridge he has recorded four other centuries in England – 136 at Headingley in his first Test in England in 1989, 124 at Old Trafford and 111 at Lord's, both in 1993, and 129 at Edgbaston in 1997. His best tour of England was in 1989, when he amassed 839 runs in Tests (av. 83.90) and during that particular tour he scored 1,669 runs (av. 57.55) overall. Since retiring he has been notably involved in television commentary.

Eight

Tough as Waugh 1993 to 1997

Born in the Canterbury district of Sydney
in 1965, Stephen Waugh is a right-handed
all-rounder and the current Australian
captain. He has played 18 Tests in
England, accumulating 1,312 runs (av.
69.05) with a top score of 177 not out at
Headingley in 1989. He has bagged
4 wickets (av. 91.50), with a best haul of
2 for 45 at Kennington Oval in 1993 and
he has held 13 catches. In addition to his
highest score, he has recorded five further
Test centuries in England – 152 not out at
Lord's in 1989, 157 not out at Headingley
in 1993 and 116 and 108 at Old Trafford
in 1997. Waugh played county cricket in
England for Somerset 19 times between
1987 to 1988. His career-best score was his
216 not out for New South Wales versus
Western Australia at the WACA Ground,
Perth, when he shared a record fifth
wicket partnership with his younger twin
brother Mark. The stand of
464 unfinished, was the highest
partnership for any wicket in domestic
Australian cricket. He is an avid collector
of cricket memorabilia.

Brendon Julian, nicknamed 'BJ', has played 2 Tests in England. The Western Australia left-handed all-rounder scored 61 runs (av. 30.50) with a top score of 56 not out at Trent Bridge in 1993, bagged 5 wickets (av. 58.20) with a best haul of 2 for 30 at Old Trafford in 1993 and he held 2 catches. Julien was overseas player for Surrey in 1998 after Carl Rackemann had recommended him as his overseas replacement.

The Australian touring team of 1993. From left to right, back row: E. Alcott (physiotherapist), S.K. Warne, M.J. Slater, T.B.A. May, P.R. Reiffel, M.G. Hughes, M.K. Walsh (scorer), B.P. Julian, M.L. Hayden, M.E. Waugh, D.L. Martyn, W.J. Holdsworth, R.B. Simpson (coach). Front row: T.J. Zoehrer, S.R. Waugh, M.A. Taylor (vice-captain), A.R. Border (captain), D. Rundle (manager), D.C. Boon, C.J. McDermott, I.A. Healy.

Victorian right-arm medium pace bowler Paul Reiffel, nicknamed 'Pistol', played 7 Tests in England. He scored 241 runs (av. 40.17) with a top score of 54 not out at Headingley in 1997, and he took 30 wickets (av. 22.97) with best haul of 6 for 71 at Edgbaston, in 1993 and he held 2 catches. Reiffel played a season of county cricket for Nottinghamshire in 2000.

Victorian leg-break wizard bowler Shane Warne has played 12 Tests in England. He has scored 301 runs (av. 23.15), with a highest score of 53 at Old Trafford in 1997, and has bagged 58 wickets (av. 25.06) with a best haul of 6 for 48 at Old Trafford in 1997. He has also held 6 catches. Warne played county cricket for Hampshire in the 2000 season.

Right-handed opening batsman Michael Slater played 6 Tests for Australia in England. He scored 416 runs (av. 41.60), with a top score of 152 at Lord's in 1993 and he held 2 catches. Slater has played county cricket in England for Derbyshire and has acted as a television commentator in 2000 for Channel 4.

Mark Waugh, the twin brother of Stephen, was born in the Canterbury district of Sydney in 1965. The right-handed New South Wales' all-rounder has played in 12 Tests for Australia in England. He has amassed 759 runs (av. 39.95), with a top score of 137 at Edgbaston in 1993, and he has held 15 catches. His best bowling performance was 1 for 16 at Kennington Oval in 1997 and he has taken 2 wickets (av. 88.50). Waugh played county cricket in England for Essex in 65 matches between 1988 and 1992 thanks to Allan Border recommending him to the Chelmsford-based county club. He accumulated 2,072 runs (av. 76.74) for Essex in 1990. His career-best score was his 229 not out for New South Wales versus Western Australia at the WACA Ground, Perth, when he shared a record fifth wicket partnership with his brother.

Justin Langer, nicknamed 'Alfie', toured England in 1997 but did not play in any Tests. He has since played two seasons of county cricket for Middlesex from 1999 to 2000. During the latter season he took over as captain from Mark Ramprakash.

A fully printed up scorecard for the Kent versus Australia tourist match which took place at St. Lawrence Ground, Canterbury on 16, 17 and 18 August 1997. The Australians were victorious by the margin of 6 wickets.

TOURIST MATCH

KENT v AUSTRALIA Canterbury - August 16th 17th 18th 1997

SCORE CARD 40p

Hours of Play: 1st & 2nd day 11.00 - 6.30 p.m. 3rd day 11.00 - 6.00 p.m. * Captain
Intervals: Lunch 1.15 (3rd day 1.00); Tea (usually) 4.10 (3rd day 3.40) + Wicket-keeper
Umpires: J. Holder and M. Harris   Scorers: J.C. Foley

Kent won the toss and elected to bat

KENT

		1st Innings		2nd Innings	
1	T.R. Ward	ct Berry b Kasprowicz	0	ct Blewett b Bevan	66
2	E.T. Smith	ct Lee b Kasprowicz	0	lbw b M. Waugh	46
3	A.P. Wells	ct Berry b Kasprowicz	0	ct Berry b Young	65
4	A.P. Igglesden	ct Berry b Lee	0	not out	2
5	W.J. House	ct Langer b Kasprowicz	16	b Lee	20
6	M.A. Ealham	ct S. Waugh b Bevan	30	ct Ponting b Kasprowicz	85
7	M.V. Fleming	ct Berry b Lee	67	ct Berry b Lee	29
8	P.A. Strang	ct Langer b Lee	0	ct Ponting b Lee	2
*9	S.A. Marsh	not out	35	ct Kasprowicz	5
10	B.J. Phillips	ct M. Waugh b Young	25	ct S. Waugh b Kasprowicz	0
11	J.B. Thompson	ct Ponting b Lee	0	ct Ponting b Kasprowicz	3
12					
	Extras	B - L/B - 2 W - NB - 26	28	B - 4 L/B - 2 W - NB - 12	18
		Total -	201	Total -	343

Runs at fall of wicket
1st Innings 1-2 2-6 3-15 4-46 5-77 6-107 7-197 8-201 9-201 10-
2nd Innings 1-99 2-159 3-200 4-233 5-234 6-285 7-303 8-307 9-318 10-

Bowling Analysis	Overs	Maidens	Runs	Wickets
Kasprowicz	15	4	52	4
Young	11	3	46	1
Lee	10.3	4	27	4
Bevan	11	4	49	1
Blewett	3	1	5	0

Bowling Analysis	Overs	Maidens	Runs	Wickets
Kasprowicz	24	4	89	3
Young	15	7	40	1
Lee	25	7	86	4
Blewett	5	2	26	0
M. Waugh	12	5	30	1
Bevan	17	2	66	1

AUSTRALIA

		1st Innings		2nd Innings	
1	M.J. Slater	lbw b Igglesden	14	b Fleming	47
2	J.L. Langer	ct Marsh b Igglesden	20	ct Marsh b Thompson	22
3	G.S. Blewett	run out	0	ct Marsh b Thompson	18
4	M.E. Waugh	c Marsh b Igglesden	1	c Smith b Strang	35
*5	S.R. Waugh	c Marsh b Strang	154		
6	R.T. Ponting	b Ealham	32	not out	56
7	M.G. Bevan	c Ward b Phillips	55	not out	47
8	S. Young	c Marsh b Phillips	0		
9	S. Lee	c Marsh b Phillips	1		
+10	D. Berry	c House b Thompson	12		
11	M.S. Kasprowicz	not out	12		
12	M.T.G. Elliott				
	Extras	B - 7 L/B - W - 1 NB - 6	14	B - L/B - 2 W - NB - 4	6
		Total -	315	Total -	231

Runs at fall of wicket
1st Innings 1-29 2-31 3-35 4-40 5-106 6-264 7-266 8-268 9-288 10-
2nd Innings 1-67 2-91 3-95 4-141 5- 6- 7- 8- 9- 10-

Bowling Analysis	Overs	Maidens	Runs	Wickets
Igglesden	16	2	56	3
Phillips	15	1	57	3
Ealham	13	3	63	1
Thompson	11	1	61	1
Strang	20.1	4	44	1
Fleming	5	0	27	0

Bowling Analysis	Overs	Maidens	Runs	Wickets
Igglesden	5	1	28	0
Ealham	5	1	19	0
Phillips	6	2	36	0
Thompson	12	3	58	2
Strang	11	1	22	1
Strang	10	0	42	1
House	2.5	0	24	0

(Minimum overs in the day will be 98 except for the last day which will be a minimum of 75 overs)

126

Left: Glenn McGrath has toured England once in 1997. He played in all 6 Tests of the summer and bagged 36 wickets (av. 19.47), with a best performance of 8 for 38 at Lord's when England were dismissed for just 77. He scored 25 runs (av. 12.50), with a top score of 20 not out at Headingley, and he held 2 catches. In 2000 he played for Worcestershire. *Right:* Tasmanian right-handed middle order batsman Ricky Ponting has toured England once in 1997. He played in 3 Tests during the summer and scored 241 runs (av. 48.20), with a highest innings of 127 at Headingley, and he held a single catch.

Michael Bevan toured England in 1997, playing in 3 Tests. He scored 43 runs (av. 8.60), with a top score of 24 at Edgbaston, and he took 2 wickets (av. 60.50), with a best of 1 for 14 at Headingley, when his left-arm spin deceived Mark Butcher, who was stumped by Ian Healy for 51. He held a single catch. In 2000 he played for Sussex.

Left: Matthew Elliott, the tall left-handed Victorian opening batsman, toured England in 1997 and he played in all 6 Tests of the series. He amassed 556 runs (av. 55.60) with 2 hundreds and 2 fifties and he held 4 catches. His highest innings in Tests were 199 at Headingley, 112 at Lord's, 69 at Kennington Oval and 66 at Edgbaston in his first Test in England. Elliott represented Glamorgan as overseas player during the 2000 season. *Right:* Right-arm quick bowler Jason Gillespie toured England in 1997 and he played in 4 Tests. He bagged 16 wickets (av. 20.75), with a best haul of 7 for 37 at Headingley, and he scored 57 runs (av. 11.40), with a top score of 28 not out at Old Trafford and he held 3 catches.

The Queensland right-arm pace bowler Michael Kasprowicz toured England in 1997 and played in 3 Tests. He bagged 14 wickets (av. 22.14), with a best performance of 7 for 36 at Kennington Oval, in the Sixth Test of the series, despite England winning that Test by the small margin of 19 runs. He scored 21 runs (av. 5.25), with a highest score of 17, at Edgbaston, and he held 2 catches. Kasprowicz has played county cricket in England for Essex and Leicestershire.